# My HOMESTEADER'S Heritage

Laurence Croswell

# MY HOMESTEADER'S HERITAGE
Copyright © 2016 by Laurence Croswell





ISBN: 978-1-4866-1328-1

Word Alive Press
131 Cordite Road, Winnipeg, MB R3W 1S1
www.wordalivepress.ca

Library and Archives Canada Cataloguing in Publication

Croswell, Laurence, author
      My homesteader's heritage / Laurence Croswell.

Issued in print and electronic formats.
ISBN 978-1-4866-1328-1 (paperback).-- ISBN 978-1-4866-1329-8 (ebook)

      1. Croswell family.  2. Stebner, Ed.  3. Stebner, Ed--
Family.  4. English--Prairie Provinces--Biography.  5. Polish people--
Prairie Provinces--Biography.  6. Immigrants--Prairie Provinces--
Biography.  7. Frontier and pioneer life--Prairie Provinces.  8. Prairie
Provinces--Emigration and immigration--History. 9. Prairie
Provinces--Biography.  I. Title.

FC3239.R3C76 2016            971.2'020922            C2016-902829-1
                                                     C2016-902830-5

# Contents

# *Acknowledgements*

*My Homesteader's Heritage* began about forty years ago when interest in my family's roots was piqued by Chuck Nelson, who began to research the Croswell family and their immigration from England to Upper Canada in 1842. My son, Mark, joined me in collecting more information about the Croswell clan from family papers and letters. Phil Hosick, whose paternal grandmother was a member of the Croswell family, provided valuable information from his research for his university papers; moreover, his home was in Ahmic Harbour, where many of the early Croswell settlers resided. As far as I know, My *Homesteader's Heritage* is the first formal publication to record our Croswell ancestry

The Stebner history research was conducted more recently. My son, Mark, who is a history teacher at Bayview Secondary School in Richmond Hill, Ontario, initiated research into the origins of his Stebner ancestors who were members of a German settlement living in Poland during World War I. My grandmother, Helen Stebner, provided me with the anecdotes about life during the war. My mother, Ella, vaguely recalled the trip across the ocean and arriving at Pier 21 in Halifax; her memories of homesteading in Newbrook were more vivid.

It has been an honour to write this short history about the two sides of my family, the Croswells and Stebners. My nuclear family has supported me for forty years as senior pastor of Centennial Road Standard Church. Without them this story could not have been written. I have a loyal wife, Faye, two terrific sons, Mark and Darren, two marvelous daughters-in-law, Lauri and Shannon, and now the joy of my life, grandchildren: Austin, Abigail, and Sadie ... and hopefully more to come! You are the greatest family, and I love you!

# CHAPTER ONE

# New Worlds Calling

Leave your country, your relatives, and your father's
home, and go to a land that I am going to show you.
—Genesis 12:1 (GNT)

"Rebecca Hobbs may have been the old woman who lived
in a shoe with so many children she didn't know what
to do. Rebecca cared for twenty-four in her lifetime!"[1]

Rebecca Hobbs is my great, great grandmother. The Parish register, Kingsworthy, Hampshire, records that in 1810, "Rebekah, daughter of William and Mary Hobbs, born July 10 was baptised July 29." Rebecca (notice different spelling), the second youngest daughter, was not the first girl to bear her name in the family, but apparently inherited her sister's name, born previously, who sadly died in infancy.[2] It was a morbid tradition, but often when a child died, the next born of the same sex would inherit the dead child's name.

---

1 Mark Croswell, Legion Public Speaking Contest, Lyn, Ontario, 1986.

2 Rebecca Hobbs, born May 1806, Christened May 22, 1806, Kingsworthy, Hampshire, England, cited by Chuck Nelson from information by Audrey Gledhill, 1103 Hansard Cres., Coquitlam, BC, V3C 4W2.

Page 36.

MARRIAGES solemnized in the Parish of _Micheldever_
in the County of _Southampton_ in the Year 18_28_

_Charles Croswell_ of _this_ Parish

and _Rebecca Hobbs_ of _this_ Parish

were married in this _Church_ by _Banns_ ~~with Consent of~~
this _seventeenth_ Day of
_April_ in the Year One thousand eight hundred and _twenty eight_
By me _Thos. Clarke Vicar_

This Marriage was solemnized between us { ~~Charles Croswell~~
The mark X of Rebecca Hobbs

In the Presence of { _William Cook_
_William Lipscomb_

No. 106.

_William Walker_ of _this_ Parish

Church Register
St. Mary the Virgin Church of England
Record of marriage: Charles and Rebecca Hobbs, April 17, 1828

Rebecca was seventeen when she married Charles Croswell on April 17, 1828. The Reverend Clarke, Vicar of St. Mary the Virgin Church of England in the Parish of Micheldever, Hampshire, England, officiated at the marriage ceremony.[3] Unlike many of the poor, Charles and Rebecca had scraped together the shilling that a proper ceremony required; many of the poor simply set up house together in common-law arrangements, or plighted their troth before an old family friend. Rebecca was obviously illiterate, since she signed her name in the church register with the mark of an "X" (few girls attended school in those days). Charles was at least partially literate, for his signature is recorded in legible,

---

3 _Register: Marriages Solemnized in the Parish of Micheldever in the County of Southampton_, 1828, 36.

but visibly forced, handwriting. Little is known of the early life of Charles, other than he was born in 1800 in Saint John, Portsea, Hampshire and named after his father. His mother was Catherine Croswell.

Micheldever to this day is a picturesque village situated between Winchester and Basingstoke, England, in what is primarily a farming community. Both the Croswell and Hobbs families were likely brick makers and subsistent farmers in the peaceful countryside of Southern England.

Soon after marriage, Charles and Rebecca were drawn by the lure of employment opportunities available in the smog-filled city of Leeds. The two newlyweds settled down to eke out a living among the roaring factories and damp tenements of the crowded city, one of the earliest cities of England to be transformed by the Industrial Revolution. Family historian Phil Hosick[4] explains that work was available for anyone willing to toil long hours for pittance wages—unfortunately, the only choice for the uneducated masses. But as the population burgeoned, so did the squalor on the streets. Raw sewage, if not dumped on the sidewalks, poured into the waterways. Drinking water teemed with E. coli, salmonella, and cholera bacteria. Disease was rampant. Small pox, cholera, and various other plagues claimed the lives of better than ten percent of the children who survived birth. Misery was everywhere. Charles and Rebecca learned early to cope with hardship and heartache.[5]

According to most records, it was in this industrialized city of Leeds that Charles and Rebecca's eight children were

---

4 Phil Hosick is the great, great, great grandson of Charles and Rebecca Croswell on two lines of his family tree; his father's parents were second cousins and both great grandchildren of Rebecca and Charles.

5 Phil Hosick, *An Essay on the Life of Rebecca Hobbs*, Queen's University, 2001

born.[6] However, one source lists William (my great grandfather) as being born in Hampshire, England, on April 22, 1830. Another source indicates his younger brother, John, also being born in Hampshire. We're unsure why this discrepancy exists between Leeds and Hampshire as the places of birth—perhaps a clerical error, or a temporary move back home, or the Charles Croswell family moved from Hampshire after the three oldest boys were born. At any rate, Charles and Rebecca eventually migrated to permanently live and work in the industrialized city of Leeds. They exchanged the peace and serenity of the County of Hampshire for the squalor and pollution of what they hoped would be the economic advancement of Leeds.

Life in Leeds was stifling with fewer opportunities for material or social advancement than supposed. To survive, every able-bodied member of the family had to work. Children were not treated well in the factories, although thanks to the Factory Act of 1833, children aged nine to thirteen were only allowed to work eight hours daily. Little wonder that many of the hard pressed labourers were tantalized by rumours of life in North America. There were stories of boundless opportunities to prosper, along with promises of fresh air and wide spaces to grow. Such enticing news and promises filtered back to Charles and Rebecca. Uprooting to Canada made sense to the ever-growing Croswell brood, and they longed for a new start and the economic advantages in the land of opportunity across the ocean. By the end of 1841, the Croswells had scrimped and saved enough to purchase fares on a sailing vessel bound for the frontiers of Canada.

---

6 Charles Jr. (1829); William (1830); John (1831); Benjamin (1833); Doretta (1834); Rebecca (1835); Cornelius (1837); infant Stephen (1841)

## FAREWELL, MOTHER ENGLAND!

During the spring of 1842, the Charles Croswell family made their way to the seaport of Liverpool, where they obtained passage tickets from one of the passenger brokers with whom they could bargain the best deal. Competition was brisk, and fares varied from three pounds, ten shillings to five pounds on any given day. Immigrating passengers were lucrative cargo for ships that had lost their African slave trade and saw passenger service to the New World as a way to fill their holds on their outward journey to return with Canadian lumber. There is no record on how well Charles and Rebecca bargained. Statistics provided in 1842 indicate that the Croswell family joined over 54,000 British subjects who sailed to the North American colonies and nearly 64,000 to the United States.

The sailing ships for the most part were built for a maximum passenger load of 165, but many set sail with up to 276. Unfortunately, the name of the ship the Croswell family boarded was not documented and has been forgotten. An excerpt from *The Passenger Act* passed about that time and quoted in an 1850 issue of the *Illustrated London News* stated:

> No passenger ship is allowed to proceed until a medical practitioner appointed by the emigration office of the port shall have inspected the medicine chest and passengers, and certified that the medicines are sufficient, and that the passengers are free from contagious disease ... when the emigrant and his family have undergone this process, their passage-ticket is stamped, and they have nothing further to do, until they go on board, but to make their own private arrangements and provide themselves with outfits, or

with such articles of luxury or necessity as they may desire over and above the ships allowance.[7]

We can only imagine the frenzied scene in the crowded port of Liverpool—a young family with eight children: Rebecca, an infant in her arms; Charles Jr., the oldest son at thirteen, assisting his father to keep the family together . . . they mingle with the perspiring throngs of pushing people, bargaining for passage tickets, attending to last minute details, transporting their life possessions in trunks and leather bags . . . bedding under arm . . . ready for boarding. Finally, the Croswells join the jostling line leading up the steep gang plank to the waiting ship that would soon sail for a land they'd never seen. They were leaving the country of their forefathers, the country of their birth, the country of their childhood—their home, despite its hardships and constant battles—forever.

An early account of ship departures tells of throngs of spectators watching from the shores as the huge sailing vessels were towed out: "Hats are raised, handkerchiefs are waved, and a loud and long-continued shout of farewell is raised from the shore, and cordially responded to from the ship."[8]

## CRUEL HAND OF ADVERSITY

The voyage to Canada in early spring was long and treacherous. Most crossings took an average of six to eight weeks, weather permitting. However, menacing icebergs drifting into the cold Labrador Current delayed progress of the Croswell vessel. The voyage was fraught with danger. Conditions were cramped as passengers held fast to the trunks and bags containing their

---

7 Passenger Act, 12 and 13, Vict., c.33; cited by Phil Hosick
8 *London News*, Saturday, July 6, 1850, cited by Phil Hosick

meagre worldly wealth. To keep costs down, bunks were narrow and tiered with little more than a few wooden slats and a thick layer of straw between them; passengers usually shared bunks and took turns sleeping. Holds were dungy and dark. As the voyage slowly continued, food began to rot from lack of refrigeration and the extended travel time on the ocean. Much of what was cooked was not properly prepared by the ship's galley crews. Menus were nutritionally inadequate: hard biscuits, stale bread, oatmeal, molasses, rice, sugar, and a measured amount of contaminated water daily[9]—insufficient to maintain health or resist disease. Moreover, as the sailing stretched into weeks, the ship became seriously short of provisions. Not surprisingly, an epidemic of ship's fever (cholera) broke out on board the dingy wooden sailing vessel. Many of the passengers and crew succumbed to the dreaded disease. Dysentery and vomiting added a foul stench to the ship during the thirteen weeks it took to cross the iceberg infested Atlantic. Crew and passengers succumbed to death as travel became an ordeal of survival.

It's probable that each one of the Croswell passengers suffered effects from the illness aboard the ship, but the first one to succumb was baby Croswell, still a nursing infant. Accounts reveal that burial at sea was a crude ceremony: the body of the infant would be wrapped in a strip of canvas, weighted with perhaps a link of chain. After a short and simple prayer, the body was placed on a plank and tipped overboard into the frigid Atlantic waters.

Another victim of the cholera epidemic was, like Rebecca, a young mother of eight, also nursing a baby. Her name was Mary French. She and her husband, George, had embarked on the same journey with the same aspirations and hopes as the Croswell family. It's probable the two families had become

---

9 Ibid.

acquainted on board the ship, and now George was a grief stricken widower with a nursing baby. His plight didn't go unnoticed by Rebecca, still grieving the loss of her infant to the watery grave. Despite her own pain, Rebecca offered to nurse the French baby to save the little girl's life. Little did Rebecca know how the hand of fate was at work pulling and joining the Croswell-French families together.

Three days from the shores of Canada, "Rebecca's worst nightmare came true . . . her own husband, Charles, having suffered the withering effects of cholera, died."[10] One can only imagine the scene of sorrow and loss. What options were open to a thirty-two year old mother with seven children under fifteen years of age? Moreover, she was nursing a motherless infant.

Fortunately, the Croswell ship was within three days of landing at the quarantine station of Grosse Isle, some thirty miles (forty-eight kilometres) east of Quebec City. Grosse Isle was the Canadian immigration point and depot set up in the Gulf of St. Lawrence in 1832 to contain diseased immigrants to British North America. Custom dictated that victims were spared the watery grave and were buried on Canadian soil. Logistics suggest Charles was buried at Grosse Isle, saving Rebecca and family the horror of watching Charles slip into an unmarked water grave at sea.

## NEW WORLD

With few resources, their meagre savings mostly used up, and no desire to face the horrors of another horrendous ship ride back to England, Rebecca and family decided there were few options but to press on to their planned destination—Upper Canada. Furthermore, their new found friendship with the

---

10 Ibid.

French family formed a partnership of security and gave them courage to continue their journey together. Thus, after passing quarantine at Gross Isle, both families set out on the next leg of travel—the journey up the St. Lawrence River. Family tradition says they disembarked at Montreal and continued by barge and steamboat into the wilds of Lake Ontario.[11] Finally they docked, unloaded all their trunks and baggage on the western edge of Lake Ontario, and found lodging in Dundas, a bustling town near the present-day city of Hamilton. After weeks of planning, packing, sailing, suffering, hardship, and loss, they had arrived!

George French had been especially kind and helpful to Rebecca and her family; Rebecca Croswell had been sympathetic and caring to the French family. Rebecca's oldest son, Charles (fourteen years of age as of July 5), was not yet capable of supporting his mother and six younger siblings; George French's eldest daughter, Anne, was too young to care for her father and her seven younger siblings, which included a nursing baby. The practical prevailed. After some consideration, widower French and widow Croswell decided to marry. The wedding took place that fall on November 10, 1842.[12] The marriage was not, insists the family, one of simple convenience, but one of sympathy, mutual respect, and affection.

---

11 Lynda Lee French, *George and Rebecca Hobbs Croswell French.*

12 Cited in Roots Web's World Connection Project: *Additions and Corrections to a Prairie Family's Past* (1982): McMaster University Archives, Diocese of Niagara fonds, Box 154, Records of St George's Church, Guelph, Parish Register B, "Marriages during 1842": #13, Married this tenth day of November 1842 after due publication of Banns, George French of the township of Guelph (Widower) and Rebecca Crosswell of the same Township (Widow) by me, Arthur Palmer," Rector of Guelph. The marriage was solemnized between us; "George French" and Rebecca French (X her mark).

Thus began a new era in the Croswell-French saga. The newlyweds began with a joint family of fifteen, all in a weakened state from their horrendous ocean trip. The large blended family continued to live in the vicinity of Dundas for the next five years. Like Rebecca's first husband, George was also a brick and shingle maker by trade; it's likely that he and his older sons and stepsons employed these trades in Dundas to earn money to purchase farming tools and equipment needed to begin producing crops. Whether they rented land or were able to purchase is unknown, but the land was suitable for farming. With their trade as brick and shingle makers, the family was able to make ends meet.

The first five years of life in Canada were probably the most difficult. The goal was survival: find employment, build a shanty to accommodate a family of fifteen, find fuel for stoves, provide food for hungry mouths, and scrounge for clothing to endure the cold winters. They faced emotional hardships: isolation, loneliness, separation from families and friends in England, adjustment to a new culture and way of life, and fears for the future in a wild and primitive country. Roads, canals, and railroads were limited and provided limited communication and transportation of goods. Success was determined by hard work, endurance, and sheer grit. By 1847, George acquired the right to settle in Peel Township on Lot 15, Concession XVI, and the prospect of farming one hundred acres of land brightened prospects for the family.

Soon Rebecca and George began to produce a third family. The first child born to this new union was James, on March 10, 1844. Seven more were born in quick succession.[13] Rebecca

---

13 Children born to Rebecca and George: James (1844); Frederick (1845); Charlotte (1846); Sophia (1848); Benjamin (1850); Phoebe (1851); Isaac (1852); Henry (1856).

Rebecca Hobbs Croswell French became mother to twenty-four children, and grandmother to more than one hundred.

cared for a total of twenty-four children, including Baby Croswell who was buried at sea.

## BLAZING TRAILS

The Croswell-French clan had always dreamed of taking ownership of a farm, but as the Dundas area was filling up with immigrants from Scotland, Ireland, and England, land became more difficult to obtain. Moreover, with so many immigrants arriving, the cholera epidemic soon spread to the nearby cities of Toronto and Galt and was in danger of spreading to Dundas. It made sense, then, that when Upper Canada released

Clergy Reserves[14] for general settlement, George and Rebecca would decide to move their family north to claim a homestead of cheap government land in the virgin bush of Peel Township. They loaded their possessions and made their way north by horse, oxen, and wagon to Fergus; the final leg of the journey was only a "blaze through the bush." Upon arriving, it seems from family reports that "the clan" lived as squatters for a period, not taking legal possession of the land until 1847.[15]

The Croswell-French family lived together, clearing and breaking the soil. The land was flat; the clay loam was rich and productive—crops flourished. Moreover, they discovered clay beds suitable for brick making. By 1850, when George French was about fifty-four, it appears that he decided to leave the hard farm work to his sons and stepsons, while he concentrated on making bricks and shingles.[16] The business did well, for many schools, churches, and homes were sheaved with French bricks.

The Croswell-French family were neighbours and friends of the Larmers, an Irish family from Belfast, Northern Ireland, that had arrived about 1845, just before or near the beginning of the wave of Irish Catholic immigrants suffering from the potato famine of 1846–1851. The Larmers, like thousands of other Irish, were seeking greater opportunity on the other side of the Atlantic. James Larmer, whose wife, Martha, had died previously in Ireland, was a widower with three daughters and one son. Their ship had been stuck in icebergs for four days, and daughter Christina, who was about fifteen years of age at the time, remembered the porpoises surfacing in

---

14 Clergy reserves were tracts of land reserved for the support of "Protestant clergy," interpreted to mean the Church of England.

15 Research by Robert Merrill Black, *The Croswell History*, 1982 : Lot 15, Concession XVI, Wellington County.

16 Ibid.

the water and rolling around the ship. The Larmers, like the Croswell-French clan, had made their way to Dundas to settle and find work. Eventually, four from the Croswell family were united in marriage to each of the four Larmer children.[17] There were no dating agencies, but why go searching afar when a compatible mate lives just a few miles down the road?

## RELIGIOUS AFFILIATION

Two Croswell-Larmer weddings are recorded in the register of St. John's Anglican Church, Elora: Charles Croswell and Christina Larmer, February 14, 1850; and John Croswell and Sarah Larmer, June 6, 1851. There are no later references to Croswell-French marriages or baptisms. Furthermore, since the Wellington County Atlas identifies George French as a Methodist, it's likely the switch was made to that denomination in the early 1850s.[18] It was during the mid-nineteenth century that the Methodist revivals with their ubiquitous circuit riders and evangelists swept through Ontario, converting thousands to faith and bringing them into the membership of the Methodist Church. It's reported that George helped build Mount Hope Mission House for homeless squatters who had fled slavery from the American South along the Underground Railway.

It's obvious that some in the Croswell-French connection had a strong Christian faith, since Edith (Griffith) McDowell

---

17 Croswell Family Group Record: Charles, Rebecca's oldest son, married Christina Larmer; John Croswell married Sarah Larmer; Rebecca Croswell (daughter) married Robert Larmer; and Cornelius (Nelly) Croswell married Catherine Larmer. Sadly, it seems that Rebecca Larmer died in childbirth, for Robert Merrill Black cites in the 1861 census of Peel, Robert Larmer is married to Mary French. Provided by Chuck Nelson.

18 Unfortunately, Elora Methodist records were lost in a fire in 1910; Robert Merrill Black.

writes that her grandmother, Christina Croswell, was "raising her family as Christians should ... How well I remember," she recalls, "when we children went to her home to stay all night, she would bring the Bible and have one of us read before going to bed."

## WIDOW AGAIN

George and Rebecca's last child was Henry, born in 1856; George was sixty and Rebecca was forty-six. George began to noticeably slow down—he is listed in the census as a shingle maker, a more sedentary occupation. The County Atlas of 1906 reports: "[H]e was a Methodist and a very strong Conservative, taking a great interest in the affairs of the party." He became a staunch Conservative and lived to witness the celebration of Canada's Confederation; his death is cited as October 14, 1867, only a few months after Canada became a nation. For many years, his burial place was uncertain, but a couple of school children playing in the woods discovered a limestone marker wedged between two trees in the Drayton Cemetery a few miles from his home.[19] George was seventy-one years old.

Rebecca, now a woman of fifty-seven, became a widow for the second time: her youngest son, Henry, was eleven; her daughter, Phoebe, a teenager of thirteen; and Isaac, fifteen. Once again she and her family faced poverty. Fortunately, this time she had grown sons and daughters with better financial means to surround their mother with care and support. Her descendants report that she and her children were fed, clothed, and well-tended. Four years later, in 1871, nineteen year old Isaac and his younger fifteen year old brother, Henry,

---

19 Lynda Lee French, *French History*

took on the responsibilities of the farm, the brickyard business, and tending to their mother.

## NEW ONTARIO

The Croswell-French clan seems to have had an adventurous, pioneering spirit embedded within their genes. During the 1870s, a number of them decided to move, caravan style, from Peel Township into the wild lands being opened up in "New Ontario," the Muskoka and Parry Sound areas. They settled in Croft and Hagerman Townships, between the villages of Dunchurch and Ahmic Harbour.[20] The land was rich in heavy timber, which quickly attracted logging and lumber companies. But it was not productive farmland. Phil Hosick, whose boyhood years were spent near Ahmic Harbour, quotes from Denny's in Parry Sound: "Rock, birch, white pine, blueberries and lakes make delicious country for summer cottages, as Muskoka, Lake of Bays and Parry Sound still testify; but they don't make good farms."[21]

John Croswell was one of the first pioneers who moved to Ahmic harbour with his family and carried on the family business of making bricks in conjunction with farming. He also became the postmaster. John Macfie of the *Parry Sound North Star* has written much about him and claims that John was no amateur at the brick maker's trade:

Considering the modest size of the hole in the ground it left, John Croswell's brick making made a

---

20 Robert Merrill Black.

21 Cited by Phil Hosick: *Denneys, Lester and Orpen, The Illustrated History of Canada*, 1987, 316.

respectable mark on the landscape within a radius of several miles of Ahmic Harbour. [22]

He found a deposit of suitable clay for making bricks and began a lucrative business. As a result, during the closing decades of the nineteenth century, many homes, stores, churches, and at least one hotel in the vicinity were clad with John's bricks of orange-red hue. Of interest are some of the remaining bricks found stamped with "JC," as well as many with a backwards C (a mistake in setting up the clay mould) to identify the brick maker, John Croswell.[23]

## GRANNY FRENCH

Rebecca, now the aging family matriarch, had remained with her son, Isaac French, in the Township of Peel. Isaac, described as a "canny and prosperous farmer, raising fine horses" had erected a large brick house on a fine one hundred-acre farm.[24] He married Jane Farrelly in 1874, and soon the couple began a family of their own. By the 1880s, Rebecca, now in her seventies, craved the peace and tranquility impossible to find in Isaac's active household of young children.[25] At the invitation of family members from the north, Rebecca moved in 1885 (likely with son, James French) to Ahmic Harbour. She settled into a small cabin on the farm of her granddaughter and

---

22 John Macfie, *The Parry Sound North Star*, Wednesday, November 28, 1990, 2.

23 I have been fortunate to obtain one of these bricks, which sits on my study shelf.

24 Compiled by Robert Merrill Black, *Genealogy ... Life in the Past Lane*, 1982

25 Ibid.

husband, Doretta and Ted Taylor (Doretta was the daughter of William and Doretta Croswell, my great grandparents).

Ahmic Harbour had welcomed various families of the Croswell-French connection. Charles had become the blacksmith. Cornelius and William Jr. took up brick making. Rebecca's younger sons, the French brothers (James, Frederick, and Benjamin) lived nearby. Rebecca was surrounded by sons, daughters-in-law, and grandchildren. She had over one hundred grandchildren living both near and far. No wonder Rebecca became known as "Granny French."

Robert Merrill Black, in his compilation of stories about the Croswell-French connection, describes Rebecca as a "homebody" who enjoyed the duties of wife, mother, and grandmother, and taught her children and stepchildren to be quiet, unassuming, and respectful of other people. The younger children were sent to school, and it's thought that most of the brood of twenty-three could read. No doubt all were taught to contribute to the well-being of the family.[26] Lynda Lee French writes in her biographical sketch that despite being illiterate (common for women in Leeds), Rebecca was a capable midwife and helped many, including her own daughters and stepdaughters, deliver their babies. Rebecca smoked a clay pipe like the Irish, but she smoked herb leaves, a treatment for her asthma. On Sunday, she wore a starched white linen apron over her many skirts and petticoats for church. Granny French had numerous pockets in her skirts, which always contained candy for children.[27]

Rebecca spent her last five years in the small but comfortable Taylor farm cottage. She was the oldest person in the community and apparently enjoyed her peaceful surroundings.

---

26 Ibid.

27 As recounted by Lynda Lee French.

It's reported that she was loved by all, although she lacked the friendship and company of contemporaries who might have shared her memories and experiences. Phil Hosick summarized Rebecca's life as a

> ... kaleidoscope of emotions: from grimy Leeds, to the heartbreak of Grosse Isle, to the bustle of Dundas, to the years of backbreaking work in Peel County, to the solitude of Ahmic Harbour.

She had taken risks and made the best of difficult circumstances. Whatever the hardships, she never gave up. She sacrificed to give her children and grandchildren a better life. Many of her offspring scattered across the New World, some westward to pioneer in what later became Saskatchewan and Alberta, others to Washington Territory in the U.S.A., and many to various locations in Ontario. Rebecca had escaped the dirty city of Leeds, England, for the fresh, clean air of Canada; in doing so, she offered her descendants, which numbered in the hundreds, the potential to prosper and live a better life.

## GRATEFUL DESCENDANTS

On a sunny August afternoon in 1990, my two sons, Mark and Darren, my wife, Faye, and I were directed to Ahmic Harbour Cemetery to find the grave of Rebecca French. It was one hundred years after Rebecca had passed away. We carefully straightened up the old tombstone etched with a calla lily and read the inscription: "In Memory of Rebecca French, Beloved wife of Geo. French, died June 3, 1890, aged 79 years, 10 months and 23 days." A verse was inscribed along the bottom:

Laurence, Darren, and Mark Croswell visit the grave site of their "Granny French," August, 1990, one hundred years after her death.

*She was a tender mother here,*
*And in her life the Lord did fear.*
*We trust our loss will be her gain*
*And that with Christ she's gone to reign.*

We stood respectfully and quietly . . . softly rubbing our fingers over the engraved marker. My thoughts were transported like the puffy clouds in the sky to a former day . . . distant memories from a different century. It was like Rebecca was standing there in her white apron. I wanted to tell her, "Thank you, Granny French, for your sacrifice and love. We won't forget. We love and appreciate you. May you rest in peace." Faye snapped a picture to memorialize the occasion.

Phil Hosick described Rebecca Hobbs Croswell French as:

...eternally barefoot and pregnant . . . through tenacious perseverance, she rose above predestined squalor and poverty to become the quiet matriarch of a strong Canadian pioneering family. . . six generations removed from this resilient soul, I still feel a kinship, a pioneering spirit and desire to know more about this tough little woman. Certainly, no silver spoon graced her mouth at birth. But if a loving happy successful family count as earthly riches, Rebecca Hobbs Croswell French died a wealthy woman.

## LEGACY

Rebecca and Charles took risks by leaving England, and they faced the adversities and consequences of that decision. Rebecca lost a mate she loved, but found love again in George—someone who had set out from England with similar dreams, but suffered loss as well. Once settled in Dundas, the new couple worked to give their children a good life in a new land, and they flourished as circumstances permitted.

Many years previous, in the grey dawn of history, another couple grew restless in the city of their surroundings. His name was Abraham, and her name was Sarah. They lived amid the smog and smut of an adulterous, evil people. Abraham's sensitive spirit protested against the evil practices, not only of his home city of Ur, but also in his father's own house. At last God appeared to him and directed him to leave for a land that He would show him.

It was no small matter for Abraham to pull up roots, tear himself from his nearest and dearest, and start for a land that he did not know. Dangers lurked along the way. His faith was severely tested. Loss. Heartache. Frustration. Ultimately, we see a tottering old man nearing the century mark still clutching the dream that he would father a nation.

Abraham was faithful to his vision. Confused at times, baffled at others, he held on to God's promise of a land and a people. But when hope seemed impossible, Sarah bore Abraham a son in his old age, and the celebration that filled the old patriarch's tent made the aged pair forget their long and weary wait. Abraham called his son Isaac. His name meant "laughter," like the laughter that filled the old couple's hearts as they contemplated the outlandish improbability of holding a son in their arms apart from God's miraculous intervention.

## ROOTS ARE IMPORTANT

Rebecca and Charles give me historical roots; my family and I are the benefactors of their vision, sacrifice, and hard labour. Abraham and Sarah give me spiritual roots; Abraham is the spiritual father of all who believe (Romans 4:11); Sarah herself bore a child when she was past age, because she judged God faithful (Hebrews 11:11). Quite a pedigree, I'd say!

# Chapter Two

# Go West, Young Man

After the death of Moses, the Lord said to Joshua
..."Now then, you and all these people, get ready to
cross the Jordan River into the land I am about to
give them . . . as I promised Moses . . .I will never
leave you nor forsake you."

—Joshua 1:1–2, 5b

## GREAT GRANDFATHER WILLIAM

William Croswell, the second son of Charles and Rebecca, was born on April 22, 1830. He is my great grandfather. Some records report that William was born in Leeds, Yorkshire, but the records of Robert Black claim William was born in Kingsworthy, Hampshire. This seems more plausible; in fact, Robert Black also records that John, the next son, was also born in Hampshire.[28] A later date for moving to Leeds would have given Charles and Rebecca time to begin their family, face economic realities, and explore the advantages of migrating to

---

28 Robert Black, *A Prairie Family's Past* (Additions and Corrections, 1982); see also Chapter 1.

Leeds. At any rate, early in their marriage Charles and Rebecca moved from the quiet countryside of Hampshire, and William spent his childhood in the grimy hustle and bustle of Leeds.

In 1842, William, at age twelve, immigrated with his parents to the British colony of Canada. His memories of the hardships in Leeds would have faded in the distant past as he began a new life pioneering in the wilds of Canada. He settled with his mother and stepfather, George French, and their large merged family in Leeds, Peel Township, in what had recently been known as Upper Canada. Under the tutelage of his stepfather, William, like his is father before him, became a brick maker and carried on the business in conjunction with farming. In 1855, at the age of twenty-five, William married another young immigrant, Doretta Verning (they probably married in the spring or summer when she was eighteen), and the couple settled near their families in Peel Township, Wellington County.

## GREAT GRANDMOTHER DORA

Doretta Louisa Johanna Maria Verning, William's wife, was born August 22, 1836 in Hannover, Niedersachsen, Germany.[29] She was known as Dora, and is my great grandmother. Her parents, Alfred and Johanna (Behrens) Verning, were German immigrants living near Galt, Ontario, but anglicised their name to Vernon. They had two children, Doretta and Fred. When the children were still young, their father died, and Johanna remarried a man by the name of Katen. She had six more children: five girls (Charlotte, Sophie, Hannah, Mary) and one boy (Lewis).

Katen was a "bush-whacker." One day while clearing bush, a tree a fell on him and crushed and killed him. Dora's mother was a widow a second time. What would Johanna Katen

---

29 As told by Robert Black.

do? She was a German immigrant with a large family to support. Her youngest, Mary, was still a small child, so she made the difficult arrangements for her sister, Mrs. (unnamed) Robinson, to adopt Mary. Mary remembers her adopted father putting her in the buggy, drying her tears, and telling her she was going to Auntie's place to live. The Robinsons were fairly well to do and gave Mary a good home and education—schooling was not compulsory, so Mary was one of few girls who learned to read and write.

One day, when Mary was a teen, a letter arrived for her at the post office. It was unusual to receive a letter in those days. It was from her long lost brother, Lewis, who was searching for the sister he hadn't seen since she was a young girl. Mary was ecstatic to reunite with her birth family, and for a short time she went to live in the home of her half-sister, Dora, who by then was married to William and beginning a family of her own.[30]

## ON THE MOVE . . . AGAIN!

When many of the Croswell-French connection migrated to lands around Parry Sound and Ahmic Harbour, Doretta and William decided to pull up stakes and join them. It seemed an opportunity to better their economic potential with others of the clan. However, they pushed even further north through the bush to Loring where William, following the trade of his stepfather, began a brick making business.

Doretta and William were typical of pioneer couples in the mid-1800s: they raised a large family—they had fourteen

---

30 Ibid.

William and Doretta Croswell raised fourteen children,
many who scattered to homesteads across the Canadian West.

children.[31] The size of this family makes it difficult to follow
all the various twists and turns of individual family histories
and where descendants eventually settled.[32] Call it the Croswell Diaspora! Many settled in Saskatchewan and Alberta,
leaving Doretta and William to retire in their Loring home
with few of their children nearby. We know that their daughter, Sarah Lillian ("Lil") remained in Loring and married
George Rogerson; the Rogersons became known for their
tourist business with lodges and guided fishing expeditions
in the rugged hinterland. Many of Doretta and William's
sons, daughters, and grandchildren had addresses that were

---

31 Margaret (1856); Doretta (1857); Louisa (1863); William (1864); Alfred
(1866); Caroline (1868); Henry (1871); Charles (1872); Amy (1874); John
(1876); Louis (1878); Sarah Lillian (1880); Frederick (1882); George

32 Seven of William and Doretta's sons moved to Western Canada: Willy
(William Jr.) & Johnny (John) buried in Saskatchewan; Alfred (Alf), Henry,
Louis, Fred, & George buried in Alberta.

far away from the old Croswell couple who had immigrated with their parents to seek better opportunities in the new world of Canada. [33]

Each of the fourteen children married and passed down stories, memories, and folklore to their children and grand-children—these stories are difficult for one individual to obtain and coordinate, especially those of diverging family lineage and geographical locations. After the third generation, most cousins lost touch with one another; hence, most events have been forgotten and new generations are unaware of the fascinating tales of their pioneer cousins and forefathers.

## RED CHARLIE

One of Doretta and William's sons, however, had a story recalled and retold by succeeding generations. His name was Charles, but he was known as "Red Charlie." Red Charlie moved to Ahmic Harbour where his cousin, also named Charles, lived.[34] Both boys bore the name of their grandfather who had perished aboard the ship sailing to Canada. To distinguish between the two men, the cousins became known as Red Charlie (his skin and hair colouring were fair and reddish) and Black Charlie (he was of darker complexion and also was the blacksmith in the village). When Red Charlie was young, a dreadful incident maimed him for life. There are two accounts of this tragic story. The stories may vary in details, but the end result was the same: Red Charlie's foot was mauled by a bear, resulting in the eventual loss of his leg. The misfortune had a profound, never-to-be-forgotten effect on the family. *The*

---

33 William died May 12, 1905; Doretta died July 24, 1913. Both are buried in Loring, Ontario.

34 His father was John, brother of William.

*Guide Book and Atlas of Muskoka and Parry Sound Districts*, 1879, quoting the *Free Grant*, June 1877, Township of Spence, reports the story as follows:

> While two young men, sons of Mr. [William] Croswell, of the township of Croft, were looking for their cows in the woods on Monday the fourth, they saw a large bear some distance from them. A small dog which had accompanied them, on seeing the bruin immediately gave chase, but instead of making for the dog, the bear made for the young men. Seeing a cedar lodged in an ash tree, they both climbed the cedar and got into the ash tree. The bear followed them, and coming up to them, tore one of the boots off the eldest boy. The boy continued kicking; the young man succeeded in driving the bear down, but very soon the bear came back and made fresh attack. He tore the flesh from both sides of the bare foot and put his tusks through the instep of the other boot trying to drag the young man down the tree. The youngest boy broke a limb from the tree, and by using it on the bear succeeded in keeping him off, but the young men were kept in the tree from 8 am to 2 pm when the bear left them. The wound young man bound up his foot and made his way home a distance of a mile and a half.

Sarah Ellen (Croswell) Ford, sister of Black Charlie and first cousin of Red Charlie, retold the story to her son, Henry Ford[35], and since she was closely related, her account has credibility:

---

35 Henry Ford (not of Model T fame) recalls his mother retelling this story about her cousin Red Charlie

Red Charlie was hunting one day with two younger boys and shot a bear. The bear was wounded and attacked the hunters. Charlie managed to push the two boys up into a tree, but did not get high enough himself; while kicking at the bear his foot was badly mauled. Doctors in the area treated his wound with their limited knowledge of medication (this was before penicillin and antibiotics); unfortunately, gangrene set in and spread so that the leg had to be amputated at the knee. As for painkillers, neither ether nor chloroform were available for surgical anaesthesia. The only way to deaden the pain was to administer whiskey until the patient was fully drunk. Sarah recalls the whiskey was not all that successful, for she remembers hearing Red Charlie scream over a block away during the amputation.

## GRANDPA FRED AND GRANDMA NELLIE

My grandfather, Frederick (Fred), was Doretta and William's thirteenth child. Fred was one of my few family members who could not read or write. He often told the story that he only went to school one day, and that day the teacher was away. We grandchildren thought he was joking, for Grandpa was a great story teller... but we learned it actually happened! When Grandpa walked to school for his first day of class, the teacher (for reasons unknown) was absent. Grandpa never returned!

As a young man, Fred was hired in Parry Sound as a river driver. River driving called for quick, nimble men with strong muscles who with long pike poles could ride the ever-turning logs downstream, watch for spots where the logs might jam, and quickly dislodge them before the logs stacked up. Fred met a young woman in Parry Sound, Helen Foreshew (known as

Fred Croswell and Hellen (Nellie) Foreshew pledged their
wedding vows on August 14, 1907.

Nellie), daughter of Frederick and Laura Foreshew.[36] Frederick
was first mate (family tradition says he later became captain) on
the S.S. *Iroquois*, one of the many small steamships that clogged
the harbours of Georgian Bay hauling freight, passengers, and
mail. His daughter, Nellie, was musical; she played the piano,
had a beautiful singing voice, and if you asked her to hum "A,"
she could sing the note on pitch for you. She'd graduated from
Howland School near her home on Manitoulin Island and was
a young woman of culture. Helen had been engaged to a local

---

36 Frederick William Foreshew, born in England, came to Canada in 1870
and married Laura Wyman born in Uxbridge, Ontario. They lived in Shequi-
andah on Manitoulin Island in a home later known as Morden House.

teacher who tragically died. Almost in a rebound from her loss, Nellie became enamoured with Fred Croswell. He was dashing, handsome, athletic, and muscular; his jovial personality drew people to him. But Fred, unlike the young teacher, was illiterate and couldn't read a word. They married on August 14, 1907, in Parry Sound.

## YOU GOTTA HAVE A DREAM

The years between 1901 and 1913 in Western Canada were boom years. Clifford Sifton's energetic Policy of the Interior (1896–1905) for filling the "Last Best West" with farmers from eastern Ontario, the United States, and Eastern Europe transformed the Prairies. The federal government vigorously portrayed the west as "The Land of Promise." The Dominion Land Act said that any adult or head of family could claim a quarter-section of free homestead land. All he had to pay was a $10 registration fee, live on the land for six months each year, build a house, and cultivate 16.2 hectares—this must be done within three years. If the settler carried out these minimal conditions, full ownership would be turned over to him. Large numbers of prospective western settlers rode John A. McDonald's Canadian Pacific Railway, and by 1905 two new provinces—Alberta and Saskatchewan—had linked the gap between Ontario, Manitoba, and British Columbia. The Croswell-French connection knew an opportunity when they saw one, and soon a number of them joined the throngs who had taken up homesteads in Saskatchewan. The population of Saskatchewan grew from 20,000 in 1880 to 286,000 by 1906 and nearly half a million by 1911. Fred and Nellie Croswell joined the migration.

On December 31, 1904, Fred Croswell, age twenty-five, made application for a homestead in South Melfort, Saskatchewan.[37] During the winter, Fred returned to work in the lumber woods of Parry Sound to save money for his newly acquired farm; summer was spent clearing, breaking, and cropping the land as well as building a house (no more than a log shack) in preparation for permanent residency on the homestead. According to his Application for Homestead Patent, Fred's family in August, 1907, consisted of himself and his wife. Obviously, Fred and Nellie had boarded the train immediately after their wedding and chugged and shunted along the wilderness rails of Northern Ontario to their homestead in Saskatchewan. Fred joined his two older brothers, Willy (William) and Johnny (John), and their families, who had also made the trek to take up homesteads nearby.[38]

## SASKATCHEWAN, LAND OF PROMISE

Homesteaders were a hardy lot! They had unbridled optimism, but it was supported by backbreaking labour. The formula for homesteading included brushing with an axe, grubbing stubborn roots, and guiding a breaking plough behind a team of oxen or horses, all the while swatting at swarms of mosquitoes and black flies; living condition were usually minimal.

Melfort was about one hundred kilometres (sixty miles) southeast of Prince Albert and was known for its black, loamy soil and productive agricultural lands suitable for the cultivation of wheat. Fred's homestead record in 1905 reports that he'd broken five acres and that he cropped them in 1906. By

---

37 Application for Homestead Patent for NE of Sec. 18, Thp. 43, Rge 17 of 2 Meridian.

38 Willy and John are buried in Melfort and Carrot River, Saskatchewan.

1907, he'd broken five more acres, as well as cropped the previous five. Slowly the Croswell homestead was making progress, for by 1910, Nellie and Fred could report twelve new acres broke and twenty acres cropped . . . along with owning three horses and seven head of cattle! They had completed enough work on the quarter section of land to comply with the homestead requirements of the Dominion Lands Act, and on September 10, 1910, they were granted the patent for full ownership of the land.[39]

The year 1910 was a banner year for Fred and Nellie. Not only did they have full title of a productive farm, but their first child, a daughter, was born that fall on October 17. They named her after both grandmothers—Laura Doretta. The next few years were spent expanding the farm, building a house and farm buildings, and raising a family. Children were an asset on a homestead: they milked cows, cleaned barns, fed cattle, helped in the fields with plantings and harvests, picked and canned wild berries, and assisted with the babies that arrived almost every two years. My father, Leonard William, was the next to be born on June 18, 1912; eight more came along at various intervals.

## PROGRESS, PANDEMIC, PANIC

The prosperity of Saskatchewan increased steadily upward until the beginning of World War I, and Fred and Nellie Croswell's Saskatchewan farm prospered as well. When war was declared in 1914, Canadian farmers, in contrast to a world in

---

39 The Application for Patent was submitted at Prince Albert, Aug. 5, 1910, "believing the homestead requirements are complied with." The application was accepted as sufficient and signed, Sept 10, 1910 by the Local Agent of Dominion Lands for Prince Albert District.

conflict, enjoyed an era of even greater wealth: the price of wheat tripled! More children, Nellie (1914) and Walter (1915), were added to the growing family's workforce. So optimistic was Fred that he decided to purchase another farm nearby and finance the mortgage with his existing homestead, now free and clear of any encumbering debts. Three more babies arrived in quick succession—Stanley, Lois (it seems she died shortly after birth), and in 1918, baby Lottie. But in the fall of 1918, as the Great War was winding down and world peace was on the horizon, another insidious monster raised its ugly head—the Influenza Pandemic of 1918.

Influenza ravaged more people in a single year than were killed in the entire World War. Estimates range from twenty to sixty million. The scourge infected one fifth to one third of the world's entire population, and 1918 would go down as a year of unforgettable suffering and death. The flu struck Melfort. Fred worked day and night helping with the chores of his sick neighbours and friends. Many succumbed to the vicious flu and fever, including the two youngest from the Croswell home, Stanley and Lottie. The joyful Croswell household was transformed to one of mourning and death. Fred was one of the few residents remaining healthy and free of the devastating illness.

The next setback was an economic crash in 1920. Farmers had been asked to produce as much food as possible to support the war effort, and the price of wheat rose from about .80/bushel in 1913 to a fixed government price of 2.25/bushel in 1918. The world wheat market became glutted when peace returned in 1919, but now the government wouldn't set a floor for the lowest price. Farmers in debt panicked with severely depressed prices that didn't recover until 1925, but it was too late for the Fred Croswell farm in Melfort. Fred and Nellie Croswell were unable to make payments on the mortgage of their second farm, and a poorly arranged business deal meant losing both farms. Years of hard work went down the drain.

## ALBERTA BOUND

In 1922, after losing his Melfort farm, Fred learned "free range land" was available for grazing cattle in Alberta. Moved by a sense of adventure and looking for opportunity, Fred and Nellie loaded up their possessions and transported their young family, now numbering six (Mildred, born 1919; Hilda, born 1920), to Waskatneau, Alberta, and the pasture lands of nearby Long Lake. Fred's brother, Henry, and his Uncle Cornelius (Uncle "Nellie"), along with some of their families, had already settled in the area.

Laura, Leonard, Nellie, and Walter were enrolled in Waskatneau School. Leonard was muscular, strong, and athletic—he excelled in wrestling, wrist twisting, running, and jumping. His brother, Walter, was the academic. On the first day of school, the school bully informed everyone that he was the boss. Leonard replied, "Let's go outside and we'll see about that!" When they returned, the bully was no longer king of the castle—Leonard was a fighter![40] Neither he nor his siblings would be bullied.

## HOMESTEADING—BALSAM GROVE

Around 1925, Fred applied for a homestead near the rangeland of Long Lake in the community of Balsam Grove. Northern Alberta Railways had built a train track in 1914 four miles to the west, and the area was touted as one of opportunity.

---

40 Mark Croswell, Leonard's grandson, enjoyed hearing Grandpa tell this story.

Leonard Croswell rides on the horse-drawn disc harrow to
cultivate a new field ready for seeding.

Fred and his family moved in for a short time with his brother,
Louis, who lived nearby and was married to Nellie's sister,
Ethel. Fred and Nellie's last child, Charles, is listed as born in
Newbrook on May 6, 1925, so obviously he arrived before any
permanent housing was available on the homestead.

Fred took his oldest son, Leonard, to view the new homestead in 1926. But where would he start? He sighed with dis-
couragement. He wasn't young anymore, and the quarter section was a profuse mixture of heavy forest divided by a swath
of low brush and swamp; the entire land mass was criss-crossed
with dead logs and debris. The rounded hills were gray wood-
ed soil, and the low areas were brown peat land. Fred shook
his head at the challenge of clearing and breaking the land—
this farm was not level with deep, black soil like Melfort.
Leonard, fourteen years of age at the time, began to cry with
disappointment and urged his dad to keep the homestead. He
convinced his dad that they could do it! Fred succumbed to
his son's energy and ambition. Soon Leonard and Walter were

Fred Croswell proudly poses with his horses and three sons,
Leonard, Walter and Charlie. Horses provided the
power needed to farm the homestead.

chopping down trees, grubbing stumps, and clearing an area
to build two log shacks—one for cooking and eating, and another for sleeping. The work was backbreaking and difficult.
Roots were yanked and pulled, large brush heaps were piled to
be burned, and three horses were hitched to the walking plow.
Walter drove the horses while Leonard gripped the two levers
to steady the plow. It was a mixture of sweat, dawn to dusk
hours, back-breaking labour, and hordes of stinging mosquitoes. But soon a small field became ready for planting.

Meanwhile, Fred drew logs from the surrounding woods
and erected a cottage-style house on a gentle slope among
some trembling aspens (called poplars by the locals). The front
door looked over a small hollow that sloped gently to the foot
of a large gravel hill. The side of the large hill faced south and
when fertilized each year with manure from the barnyard became a perfect location for a large garden.

In the summer of 1993, I videotaped an interview with three of the remaining siblings: Nellie, Walter, and my dad, Leonard. I recorded them reminiscing about pioneer days on the homestead.

"These were happy times for our family," recalled Nellie. "Mama baked twenty-three loaves of bread at a time."

"We picked wild berries for fruit," Walter added.

"Papa shot lots of moose," Leonard humourously quipped. "We had music nights, and we all sang. Mama played the organ, and Walter and I played the guitar and violin."

"We were a happy family, and we had a wonderful father and mother," Nellie added emphatically.

Balsam Grove became a rendezvous locale for a number of the William-Doretta family. Four of their sons—Alfred, Louis, George, and Fred—acquired land in the area; many of the brothers' children settled on homesteads as well. Balsam Grove School was built from logs on the corner of "Young George"[41] and Elizabeth (Jenny) Croswell's quarter section of land;[42] the teacher, Giselle Croswell,[43] and for a time all the students except two (there were about thirty students), were inter-related to the Croswell clan. It was Croswell heaven! Nellie said, "We would try to get away with things, because Giselle was our cousin." [44]

---

41 Young George was a son of Alfred Croswell, son of Doretta and William.

42 George married Elizabeth (Aunt Jennie) Brooks.

43 Giselle Croswell was a daughter of Alfred Croswell.

44 These memories are from my video interview in 1993.

## REVIVAL IN BALSAM GROVE

In the fall of 1928, William (Bill) Burger Sr., a Christian who farmed at Good Hope, Alberta, purchased land in Newbrook, where many pioneers had come to homestead and farm. There was a spiritual vacuum in the community, and people were hungry for God. Bill Burger presented the need to the Reverend Wilber J. Jackson, who was stationed and preaching at the Good Hope Standard Church, near Fort Saskatchewan. The Reverend Jackson was an evangelist mentored by Bishop Ralph Horner of the Holiness Movement Church. In the spring of 1929, Mr. Burger arranged for the Reverend to hold church services in the log schoolhouse at Balsam Grove, across from the homestead where my father, Leonard Croswell, was brushing and breaking the land.

The revival that began in those meetings would not be forgotten for many years and would touch the entire community. The Reverend Jackson preached with great power and anointing. My dad often recalled the Reverend's first words in the little schoolhouse: "I may be a stranger to you, but I am not a stranger to God." Seventy people professed faith in that revival, including Leonard's mother, my grandmother, who came to be known in the church as "Aunt Nellie." Aunt Nellie's beautiful alto voice could be heard for many years beginning the hymns on note for the congregation.

In the summer of 1930, the first Standard Church camp meeting was held on the township line, three miles east of Newbrook, due south of Leonard and Walter's farms. About two hundred were in attendance—a large number for a pioneering community. A great preaching tent with wooden benches was pitched in a clearing; a log "cook shack" was erected to provide meals, and campers pitched their own smaller tents and slept on straw ticks. The extemporaneous preaching each evening was fervent, based on a Bible text and illustrated with stories and testimonials. Members of the congregation participated with ecstatic interjections of "Glory!" "Amen!" or "Praise the Lord!" There was a loud cacophony of exuberant voices praying simultaneously and outbursts of "holy laughter" and "dancing in the Spirit." The camp lasted ten days. Visitors and preachers gathered from distant locations, and the services were a great attraction in the Newbrook community, where there was little else to compete for attention.

Weekly church services, which had begun in the schoolhouse, were moved a mile down the road to the home of Bill Croswell. In 1931, George and Elizabeth (Aunt Jenny) Croswell donated five acres of land on the corner of their farm to build a Standard Church and parsonage, and also provide space to build simple cottages and pitch a great preaching tent during camp meeting. The Reverend and Mrs. Carson were stationed at the new church and campgrounds, and the work continued to be a strong witness for many years.

## THE GREAT DEPRESSION

In 1930, the Great Depression hit Canada hard as prices and profits plunged and the economy tanked. Money was tight. In fact, Leonard recalled that once when visitors were entertained in the Croswell home, canned prunes were served for dessert. His small sister, Mildred, innocently asked her mother in front of the company if she could have two prunes. Grandma was terribly embarrassed, and answered without hesitation, "Yes, of course you can—you can have as many as you want!" But Mildred's request for two prunes divulged the truth that during normal days, only one prune was allowed. Times were tough! No one went hungry, but neither was food wasted or discarded. Fred was also a great hunter and augmented the family diet with wild meats—venison, moose, and partridge.

## WORLD WAR TWO

Slowly the Croswell farms were becoming profitable. Cleared fields were producing crops of hay and grain, cattle were pastured, and cows were milked. Walter and Leonard purchased the adjoining quarter section of land from the Kachkowski family, immediately south of Leonard's homestead, and the two brothers worked together sharing machinery and labour. In 1939, World War II erupted, and Canada was drawn into the conflict. Farmers were deemed essential to the war effort at home, but in 1942, Prime Minister Mackenzie King called for a plebiscite asking Canadians to release the government from a pledge not to send conscripts overseas for active duty. Nearly two-thirds of Canadians supported conscription, and thereafter the government enforced compulsory service.

Walter and Leonard were aware that two young men farming together would be fair game for conscription into the armed forces. Sure enough, one day as they were labouring in their harvest fields, two policemen arrived to serve notice that one of them would be required to serve in the army and prepare for possible overseas battle. The two brothers decided that Walter would volunteer to serve; Leonard would be more able to withstand the expanded, heavy farming responsibilities since Walter had earlier suffered rheumatic fever and was left with a damaged heart valve.

In 1942, Walter volunteered for active duty in the army. He was stationed in Edmonton for training, and later in 1945 was sent to Halifax. While stationed in Halifax, Walter's regiment was scheduled to go overseas for active combat. To his surprise, he was kept back—perhaps because of medical exemption (heart valve), but also because he was deemed eligible to be released for farm duty. Walter believed it was his mother's prayers that saved him from being transported overseas into active, dangerous combat. Later that year, after three and a half years in the army, Walter received an honourable discharge and returned to his farm at Balsam Grove.

## PURSUING MARRIAGE

When Walter enlisted in the army, Leonard found himself alone. He was thirty years old, the farm was making a profit worthy of supporting a family, and he began to think of marriage and the future. That would mean finding a suitable wife. Leonard had some casual girlfriends, but none that he thought would fit the bill as a farmer's wife, or someone who would meet his mother's strong expectations as to spiritual qualifications. But there was one young maiden who caught his attention. She worked at Ekert's general store and post office in the little hamlet of Newbrook where he bought groceries and picked up mail. Her name was Ella Stebner, and Leonard began to focus attention on courting her for his wife. The story of the Stebner family and the eventual marriage of Leonard and Ella is the subject of the next chapter in the saga of my life story. I am their son!

## LEGACY

Researching my family history has taught me many lessons. For one thing, I've learned that no matter how difficult or foreboding the present or future might appear, God wants us to be overcomers and rise above any difficulty or setback. God doesn't want us to become mediocre and simply accept things as they are, but to take new ground and come out ahead. He wants us to play big and not small. Whether it's facing the challenge of a homestead, or looking into the face of a financial downturn or a Great Depression, God will provide a way through that will turn out for the good of those who love Him and are called according to His purpose (Romans 8:29). This is what it means to live by faith.

God was faithful to my grandparents, Fred and Helen (Nellie) Croswell. They were overcomers. Grandma served God faithfully from the early days of the Balsam Grove revival in 1929, and believed God would bring her husband and each of her children to Himself. For many years Grandma's prayers seemed unanswered, but she was faithful and persistent in prayer. Eventually her prayers were answered. One evening at a Balsam Grove camp meeting after an invitation was given, her husband, Fred, knelt at a bench to pray and trust God for salvation. God was honouring Grandma's faith and prayers.

After her death in 1967, God continued to honour Grandma's faith and prayers. Some years later, after I became a Standard Church pastor in Brockville, Ontario, I was invited to preach at my old home church in Balsam Grove. On that special Sunday, Pastor Lawrence Yadlowski called for testimonies. One by one, Grandma's children in attendance shared their testimonies: Uncle Walter and Aunt Alice stood first and told what God was doing in their lives; then it was Aunt Nellie and Uncle Bill's turn; my mom and dad, Ella and Leonard, were there testifying to their faith. If only Grandma could have been there in that little country church! Nevertheless, I believe she was rejoicing with the angels in heaven. To top it off, her grandson preached a message of faith that Sunday from God's Word. Grandma's legacy was living on.

The old country church where Grandma had faithfully prayed for her family, where she had testified to God's faithfulness, and where she had begun so many hymns of worship and praise, was reverberating in celebration!

# Chapter Three

# Two Sides of a Coin

One generation will commend your works to another; they tell of your mighty acts.

—Psalm 145:4

## WORLDS APART

There is an old English idiom that says there are two sides to a coin; in other words, two sides may be closely related, yet they are different. I believe that is how I would describe my family roots and heritage. My father, Leonard, represents the Croswell side; my mother, Ella represents the Stebner side. My father's family spoke English; my mother's family spoke German. I'm closely related to both, yet both are different.

Ella Stebner's family takes me back to 1914 to a village in Poland where a fourteen year old German damsel by the name of Helen Pochart lived. World War I, with all its evil atrocities, had broken out in Europe. Helen was living with her mother and father, two sisters, and two brothers when their home suddenly became a hot spot about a mile from the front lines of two vicious armies determined to destroy one another with rifles and mortars. The Pochart family hunkered down in their basement to evade the whizzing bullets overhead. The windows rattled under the din of heavy explosions on the battlefield. Advancement toward them would mean fleeing as refugees to safer ground.

Fortunately for the village and the Pocharts, the fronts moved farther away, but the battleground left behind was strewn with wreckage and dead bodies. A brewery nearby had been shot full of holes, and the liquor spilled into the ditch; villagers arrived with pails and pans to help themselves to the free spirits. Helen's father, Ferdinand, was conscripted to help bury the dead. Helen begged her father to let her assist him, and reluctantly he agreed; fourteen year old Helen witnessed a horrific scene that would be indelibly impressed upon her memory. Many years later, after she had become my grandmother, she would periodically describe to me the scene of dead soldiers slumped in every imaginable position, some still propped up facing each other, simultaneously impaled through their midsections with bayonets attached to guns. Helen should have stayed home.

When the horrific war ended in 1918, the Pochart family was among the 800,000 Germans who had settled in Poland during the Austria-Hungry Empire. The German population felt increasingly alienated in Poland and complained they were increasingly marginalized in politics and denied many rights.

## MARRIAGE AND CANADA BOUND

Helen married Edmund Stebner on April 18, 1922. They lived in Tarnufka (Tarnwke), Poland, where Ella was born on January 17, 1925, and Ervin on July 5, 1926. Neighbours and friends spoke glowingly about the opportunities and safety for Germans in the United States and Canada. Many pulled up stakes and immigrated. Edmund's older brother immigrated to the United States and settled in the Madison, Wisconsin area. Edmund and Helen decided they would follow and provide a better future for themselves and their children. However, the U.S.A. soon implemented a more restrictive policy toward immigrants from Eastern Europe, so Helen and Edmund chose Canada, where Germans had been promoted since January 1927 from "non-preferred" immigrants restricted to agricultural and domestic work to "preferred" class with no restrictions for advancement and employment.

After obtaining the appropriate documents, Edmund (Ed) went ahead in 1927 and crossed the Atlantic Ocean to get things ready for his family and procure employment. Arriving at Halifax, he took the train to Winnipeg, where he passed his civil examination on April 26,[45] and then continued to Strathcona (Edmonton). He didn't know the English language—only Polish and German. There was no one to meet him. Someone at the station was able to communicate and advised him to go on to Leduc where there were many people who spoke his language and would help him get a job. Edmund caught the train south to Leduc. Helen and her two small children stayed behind in Poland to wrap up the business of selling their house and packing their personal belongings for travel.

A year soon lapsed. Ella had become proficient in two languages, German and Polish. She was an active, energetic girl, and as she liked to tell later in life, consistently had to be removed from the ladder that led to the top branches of the family cherry tree. Helen completed the property sales, and with Ella, now three years of age, and Ervin, still not two, made ready to board the ocean liner that would steam across the Atlantic to Canada. Helen recalled the week before leaving. It was like a

---

45 Immigration Identification Card

funeral around her parents' home. Her mother and father knew Canada was a long distance away, and that they probably would never see Helen or their two grandchildren again.

The day before leaving her house, Helen noticed two men dressed as women sizing up her place and peering through the window. Helen's neighbour made light of it and said there was nothing to fear since he had a gun, but Helen was convinced she must leave before evening with her money tucked in the bosom of her dress. It was a good thing she did, for about midnight, neighbours reported twelve robbers arriving—they found only an empty house, for Helen and the children were gone.

Finally, the day of departure arrived in April, 1928. There were tears and kisses and long hugs. Helen, with two small children in hand, boarded the RMS *Arabic III*, waved one final goodbye to mother and father, and sailed for Canada.

Not far out on the rolling ocean, Helen became dreadfully sea sick. She endured the two week journey, all the while sick and nauseous and unable to eat. Illness did not relieve her from the responsibility of caring for two small children. Ella, a rambunctious three year old, continually climbed on everything nearby, including the edge of the deck's railing to peer at the ocean; Helen was continually on guard to be certain Ella did not fall. Ervin, little more than a toddler, needed constant care. This was no holiday cruise for Helen!

None too soon, the little trio arrived at Pier 21 in Halifax, the recently opened Canadian ocean liner terminal and immigration facility. They were jostled among the crowds of immigrants who had arrived in Canada, a confusing cacophony of languages and voices. One can only imagine the scene: Helen, weary from her journey, shouldering bags of luggage, holding tightly on to little Ervin's hand. Ella, an impatient and curious three year old, clinging to her mother's coat; immigration officers communicating in a foreign language (one can only hope someone could speak German or Polish); ticket agents exchanging train tickets for Canadian dollars, a new currency for Helen.

Finally, they were able to pass through customs, get their immigration documents stamped, purchase tickets, and board the passenger car waiting on the rail siding beside the pier. Helen found seats, thankfully caught her breath, and settled in for the train ride to Alberta. The train slowly jerked and jolted behind the hissing steam locomotive on the long journey across the barrens of Canada, while Helen entertained and fed Ella and Ervin and tried to recover from her nauseous sea sickness and get some sleep. Many of the immigrant travelers must have wondered what kind of country they had come to as they slowly passed through the miles and miles of bush and rocks of New Brunswick and northern Ontario. A week later, they arrived in Strathcona, travel worn and weary, but safe at their Alberta destination where they were met and driven to Leduc to be reunited with Edmund.

## FROM HOMEMAKER TO HOMESTEADER

German immigrants were industrious and most always found work. Ed found employment helping grain farmers in the fertile fields around Leduc; Helen found domestic contracts cleaning houses and washing clothes; in fact, doctors in town expressed enthusiastic approval of Helen's washing ability, for she scrubbed their clothing and white smocks spotlessly clean on her rippled scrub board. The Stebners were able to purchase a small house in Leduc and were slowly accumulating and prospering in their adopted country. Another son, Rubin, was born in 1931. Ella began school in Leduc at age seven and progressed well, learning to read and speak English, although the primary language spoken at home was German.

Helen dreamed of owning her own land and farm. Some of her acquaintances had moved to homesteads father north of Edmonton to a place called Newbrook. The cost was only a ten dollar registration fee along with minimal qualifications for clearing and cropping the land. The land title would then be transferred free of encumbrances to the homesteader. Helen and Ed were discouraged from making the move by their friend George Neiman, a successful German entrepreneur, who advised them that homesteading would be a very difficult venture; he offered to lend them money to get started on land a few miles north of the Edmonton city limits. Helen could continue her domestic work, and Ed would be hired by local farmers. But Helen was adamant that she and Ed should acquire their own farm for the bargain price of ten dollars in Newbrook. It would be a place where they could build a log house; own some cows to provide milk, butter and cheese; keep chickens for meat and eggs; plant a garden for vegetables; and pick wild raspberries, strawberries, and blueberries for fruit.

We aren't certain how the homestead was chosen, but it was a swampy 160 acres with generous portions of muskeg along the Northern Alberta Railway about two miles south of the small hamlet of Newbrook. Ed went on ahead and built a temporary shack before the Stebner family moved in with him. The floor space of the shack measured about ten feet by fourteen feet, with a loft above for sleeping. A larger house of peeled logs was soon built and plastered with mud to keep out the cold north winds. Rough, un-planed planks were installed on the floor, which was temporarily used as the kitchen and family room. Shortly an addition with only a dirt floor, a common practice in these early homes, was added to be used as the kitchen—the first section was divided into two small bedrooms. A basement cellar, covered with a trap door, was dug under the board floor to be used as a cold storage room where

Ed Stebner watches over his brood sow and piglets
nursing beside the thatched roof barn.

potatoes, garden produce, and canned sealers of fruit, vegetables, and meat were stored for winter meals. Inside, the house was plastered and smoothed over with mud and then brushed with whitewash. At times, however, the strong north winds and driving rains lashed against the logs, and the mud would wash away to the floor, requiring Ed to re-mud and re-whitewash the interior as well as repair the damaged exterior.

The little house was heated with space heaters that were fuelled by wood cut from the surrounding bush of poplars, scrubby spruce, and jack pine. Stove pipes passed dangerously through the house and over the rooftop to take away the smoke from the fire. One late afternoon, when no one was home, Ervin, now a young man, arrived home chilly and cold.

"I loaded the stove up with wood and opened the draft wide to put out as much heat as possible," he remembers. "Warming up, I decided I'd better water the cattle before dark. As I walked outside, I noticed flickers of flames on the shingles outside the chimney. I quickly grabbed a pail of water,

Loading bundles onto his horse drawn rack was back-breaking
labour for Ed Stebner during the fall threshing season.

The threshing crew called for strong, hard-working men to
pitch bundles into the hungry threshing machine.

climbed onto the roof, poured water on the fire, and managed to put out the flames. I also poured water in the stove inside the house. A couple of minutes later and the entire log house would have gone up in a blazing inferno, and everything would have been destroyed." Space heaters were very dangerous.

Times were difficult for many, and the Stebner family had moved to the homestead during the mid-years of the Great Depression that devastated world economies around the world. Nevertheless, after patches of land began to be cleared, Helen planted a garden and there was a plenteous supply of vegetables; Ed seeded crops on the small fields he had brushed and broke; hay was cut with the scythe and stacked for the livestock's winter feed; the few cows purchased supplied meat and milk.

"In today's thinking, they were tough times," recalls Ervin, "but we always had lots of milk and butter. We were never hungry, and we didn't know any better."

## SCHOOLING AND EDUCATION

When the Stebners arrived in Newbrook, Ervin was ready to begin grade one. He walked with Ella on the railroad tracks to the little log school (Polard's old house) near the post office and railroad station. There were few students in the beginning, but soon a new one room school for grades one to eight was built across the road, and more students began to attend.

The walk to school was fine in the spring and fall, but the winters were dreadfully cold. Ervin was warm, because he wore long overalls and his mother knit woollen socks, which he wore inside his felt shoes and rubbers—his feet were warm and cozy during his walks. Ella, however, was a girl and wore a dress, with long brown leggings covering her legs, and woollen socks inside small low rubbers. Her feet would become freezing cold and she would cry as she walked to and from school.

The Stebner family on their Newbrook homestead.
L to R: Ed, Helen, Ralph, Ervin, Rubin, Ella

It became especially unbearable when the Stebners moved for a time to a rented location three miles east of Newbrook where they took advantage of the hay available for their cows. One winter day, as the two Stebner children were walking home from school, Ella was picked up by a horse-drawn sleigh driven by Leonard Croswell sitting beside his mother, who was wrapped in blankets with her feet on hot stones to keep warm. Little did Ella realize as she snuggled inside the blanket and warmed her toes on the stones that this was a serendipitous ride and that someday she would marry into this family.

## GRADUATION AND CAREER

Ella finished grade eight in Newbrook. Sometimes during the coldest weather she stayed with the Kramers, but as she matured into a young woman she often stayed with the Ekerts, another German family, and helped cook for their hired men or worked in the general store and post office that they owned. After leaving school as a mature fifteen year-old, Ella decided she would look for work in Edmonton. She easily found employment cleaning homes and very much enjoyed life in the city, but her mother, Helen, didn't approve of Ella being alone and so far away in the city and told her she needed to come home. She could get a job at Ekerts' store and Mrs. Ekert would teach her to play the piano as part of her wage. After about a year, Ella dutifully but regretfully returned to Newbrook. She took the job at Ekerts' store and was paid $5 per month plus piano lessons. Her job required providing breakfast for the hired men at 6:00 a.m. each morning, as well as helping in the store for the remainder of the day; she was told she should get up to practice the piano at 5:00 a.m. Ella seldom practiced the piano at that unearthly hour!

Ed and Helen Stebner were religious people, and church was important to them. They had belonged to the Lutheran Church in Poland, but German Christians in the Newbrook community attended the Pentecostal log church situated at the north end of the town. When Ella returned to Newbrook, she too attended the small log church and made many close friends. She was baptised and became involved in the fellowship and work of the church. She even considered attending Bible College and a lifetime of service.

## CROSWELL-STEBNER MARRIAGE

Customers from miles around drove their horses, tractors, and farm trucks to Ekerts' store to purchase groceries and dry goods as well as pick up their mail. One of the customers was Leonard Croswell. He was getting to the age where he was looking for a wife, and now that Ella had grown up, despite the age difference of twelve and a half years, he was intrigued with

Fred & Nellie Croswell
Grandma is wearing her plain Standard Church uniform with
no jewelry, but Grandpa is dressed up with a fancy tie!

Fred and Nellie Croswell Family (front)
Second row L to R: Hilda, Mildred, Nellie, Laura
Back row L to R: Charlie, Walter, Leonard (note the deep tan of the farmers).

Leonard Croswell and Ella Stebner engaged to be married.

her. Not only that, but his mother liked Ella because of her church activities; Ella's mother, Helen, approved of Leonard because he was a hard working farmer, and she favoured hard working men.

One day, Leonard gave Ella a ride home from camp meeting on his bicycle, and the courtship was on. They planned their wedding date for January 6, 1943, which was Orthodox Christmas day, or "Ukrainian Christmas," as it was called around the Newbrook community. It was the middle of winter, but a very nice day considering the time of year. The wedding was held in the Newbrook Pentecostal log church and officiated by W. S. Frederick; Ella's brother, Irvin, and Leonard's sister, Hilda, were the attendants. The newly-wed couple moved in with Leonard's parents, Helen (Nellie) and Fred Croswell, until summer when they moved into a granary while their upright-log house was built, plastered with mud

Leonard and Ella took their wedding pictures in an
Edmonton studio months after the wedding.

and sided with new brick siding. It was situated on another
hill about a few hundred feet to the north, just above the Fred
Croswell home. At the time, it was a beautiful four-roomed
house complete with a front covered entrance, a cottage roof
with upstairs dormer for future expansion, and a full basement; it was heated with wood heaters and a cookstove.

A year later, a baby was expected to be born sometime
during the middle of March. Plans were made near the birth
date for Ella to stay in Edmonton with Leonard's sister, Laura;
Ella would be near a doctor and hospital for a safe delivery.
But babies often come unexpectedly! An Alberta blizzard blew
in from the north during the last week of February, drifting in
roads, and making travel with the one and half ton Ford truck
next to impassable. That's when I chose to be born—two weeks
ahead of schedule! The birth pangs were becoming serious, so

Laurence, aged two, romps with his dog, Laddie, behind the newly built, up-right log house sheathed with new brick-siding. Notice Grandma and Grandpa Croswell's rambling log house in the rear to the left.

Leonard and his son, Laurence, proudly show off their new steel-wheeled tractor. The steel lugs gave needed traction to yank stubborn roots from the earth and pull a breaking plow through the virgin land of a newly brushed field.

Dad did the only thing he could: he hitched up the team of horses to the cutter and struck out over the snow to get the resident nurse in Newbrook five miles away. Fortunately, some neighbours rescued Leonard half way to town and drove him the remainder of the distance to bring the nurse back to where the sleigh and horses were hitched. Leonard and the nurse sledded back to the farm to assist Ella. Fortunately, Grandma Croswell lived only a short distance away; she and the nurse delivered me, Laurence William Croswell, on February 27, 1944, just one day short of Grandma Croswell's birthday.

I'd like to say that I was a good baby, but I would nurse, fall asleep, wake up, and wail loudly. For a young mother of nineteen, it was frustrating—not to mention the interruption of sleep and rest for everyone in the house. For two and half months this crying continued until one day Dad's cousin, Jimmy Croswell, was visiting and heard baby Laurence crying.

"He's hungry," he said. "Mix a little corn syrup with milk and give the boy a bottle and feed him."

It was just what the doctor would have ordered. Even though I looked healthy and robust, I needed just a bit more than Mom was capable of producing to satisfy my hunger pangs. We didn't have the luxury of visits to a doctor in Newbrook— most knowledge about infant care was simply word of mouth and experience passed on from one generation to another.

## CROSWELL-HAUB MARRIAGE

Uncle Walter, Dad's brother, met Alice Haub while he was serving in the armed forces. Walter liked to tell his children about his fairy tale romance, and he kept a stack of love letters they sent each other while he was stationed in Halifax. They were married on January 25, 1944, while Walter was on a short leave, about a month before I was born. After Walter was discharged from the army, he and Alice moved in for a few weeks with Leonard and Ella while they built a small house on the farm yard of the old Kachkowski homestead, a quarter of a mile to the south, and soon began raising their own family: Sharon, Wayne, Dennis, Bonnie, and Maureen were my cousins, but because our homes were so close, we were like brothers and sisters.

## BABY BROTHER

Two and a half years after my birth, a second son was born to Ella and Leonard on November 17, 1946. His name was Marvin Cecil. The weather that fall had been warm and beautiful, so there was little angst about driving the big farm truck twenty miles along the dirt road to Radway hospital. The due date was still a week or so ahead, so Walter took the farm truck to Athabasca for a couple of days. They should have learned from my birth, for Ella's contractions began before the planned date, and an early winter storm struck simultaneously. Leonard hurried to the home of Tommy Brooks a mile away to solicit Tommy and his car to rush Ella to the hospital. The temperature dropped precipitously amid the flurry of blowing snow, and the old car started to choke and sputter as the gas line began to freeze and block the flow of gas. Boiling water was obtained from a farmer's home along the road, and finally Tommy's car transported Ella just in time for Marvin to be born safely in the small country hospital that served Thorhild County. Now I had a little brother and play mate to grow up with on the farm. It also meant we shared a room.

As we grew older, Dad renovated the attic with the dormer in the log brick-siding house. The attic room was available by climbing a ladder-type stairs from the bedroom below and was closed by a trap door to prevent heat escaping when the room was not in use. Marvin's bed was on the east side, and mine was on the west. I became very fond of the attic room, because my small table desk in front of the window overlooked our front yard and garage, and I could see any activity that was going on; as well, I could look out across the field to Uncle Walter's farm. I could also look up the road towards the Township Line and know when any truck or car was approaching along the roadway—especially if it happened to be Mom or Dad driving home from town after delivering the cream and picking up groceries from Onyschuk's (they often slipped in a small bag of candies in appreciation for shopping at their store).

I had two pets of which I was especially fond. One was a little goat who became quite aggressive with his bunting and another was a collie dog we called Laddie. I was unafraid of the goat and played along with his rough-housing, and I loved Laddie and would place my arms around his furry neck with childish affection. Both animals were my playmates until Marvin was able to ride on the back of my tricycle, and I proudly peddled my brother around the farm yard. Marvin says being the second born meant he always grew up in my shadow (hung on to the back of the tricycle, so to speak) until he graduated from school and became his own person.

## CROSWELL GRANDPARENTS

I felt especially close to both of my grandmothers. For the first five years of my life, Grandma Croswell's house was only a few steps away from our house. Grandma had a pump organ, and many times I would sit beside her on the organ bench and sing along—Grandma loved to sing. She would play her organ and sing songs like "Isn't Jesus my Lord Wonderful, Wonderful." When we came to the end of the chorus, I would sing with Grandma, "Iza seen, Erza heard," thinking that Iza and

Erza were two people rather than, "Eyes have seen, ears have heard!" I never figured out how Iza and Erza were recorded in God's Word until I was much older and sang the song out of the hymn book. Nevertheless, Grandma taught me to love music. She also helped me learn how to write letters, for when she wrote to her brother, Fred, who lived in faraway Ontario, she would also help me print a letter to Uncle Fred as well, and I'd tell him that I'd like to ride a bicycle as he did.

Grandpa Croswell was a hunter and taught me how to aim and shoot a twenty-two rifle when I was still a young boy. He was always fun to be around, and we grandchildren liked to listen to his tales of the old days in the bush, or how he caught a coyote in a snare, or shot a partridge for his dinner. Grandpa smoked cigars, and we could always tell when he was visiting, because we could smell his cigar as we entered the laneway to our house. He also chewed tobacco, but he called it *snoose*; every once in a while, when we were not paying attention, he would open his small, round container of *snoose* and stick some in our mouth and laugh as we coughed and spit out the vile juice. There was one other thing I remember about Grandpa Croswell while he still lived on our farm—he had a pet red squirrel he had captured and fed peanuts to in a wire cage. It was fascinating to watch the squirrel sit on his hind legs and shell peanuts.

Sadly for me, the Croswell grandparents moved to Edmonton when I was about five years of age, and Grandpa got a construction job tearing down old houses and buildings to prepare the lots for new houses and apartments.

## STEBNER GRANDPARENTS

Grandma and Grandpa Stebner sold their farms in Newbrook and Alpen in 1945 when I was one year old, and they purchased land in Dorenlee near Bashaw, Alberta. Another son,

Ralph, had been born in Newbrook in 1934, and the Stebner family and their three sons moved to a more fertile farm without muskeg south of Edmonton.

Prospects for the new farm were promising, but a tragedy occurred a year later that changed the Stebners' joy into mourning. Rubin, their second son, died in an unfortunate drowning accident in August of 1946 when he was only fourteen years of age. Rubin and a few other young people went for a swim in the Red Deer Lake. Everyone was having a good time when, for seemingly no reason, Rubin "cramped"—doubled over—in only eight feet of water near the shore. He became helpless to stay afloat, and efforts to rescue him by his companions and brother, Ervin, were frantic but futile.

Rubin was bright, good natured, and had done well in school. His prospects to be successful in life were promising, and he was dearly loved, especially by his mother. Grandma was beside herself with grief and felt unable to face life without this favourite son who had been so thoughtful and kind to her. For weeks, Grandma seemed unable to cope with her grief, until one night through her tears she saw a vision: Rubin reached out to Grandma with open arms and said to her, "I'm alright, Mother, I'm okay." From that moment on Grandma began to heal, for she had the hope of the Resurrection—she had faith that someday she and Rubin would be reunited forever in Heaven.

I would be amiss if I didn't share Grandma Stebner's testimony of healing. Many times she retold the story as we talked around her kitchen table over moist yellow cake with creamy icing and a cup of sweet instant coffee. While farming in Dorenlee, she became stricken with serious arthritis in her legs and feet. The arthritis had caused such sharp burning in her joints that she was unable to walk upright and would crawl on her hands and knees up the stairs to her bedroom on the second floor. One evening she sat at the bottom of the stairs, unable to make her way up to the bedroom. She began to weep, and called out to God, "Please heal me, or take me! I cannot go on!" Grandma told me that instantly she was healed and began to dance and shout (out of character for a staunch Lutheran). Grandpa, who was upstairs and had already gone to bed, was startled out of his sleep to hear Grandma shouting. He hurried downstairs to find Grandma dancing around the kitchen ... healed! The arthritis never returned.

## GIVING SPIRIT

Grandmother Stebner was one of the most generous people I've ever met. She was always giving things away: it might be cabbages from her garden to share with neighbours, or a twenty dollar bill given to someone in need.

While in their fifties, Helen and Ed purchased a house in Edmonton and moved to the city. Helen worked as a caregiver for retirees in the local St. Mary's hospital; Ed got employment as a security guard at the nearby lumberyard. The Stebner home became a blessing to grandchildren who stayed with them while attending the nearby University of Alberta. We grandchildren not only paid a pittance to rent the upstairs apartment at 10526-80th Avenue, but every so often Grandma would invite us down for a "snack" of garlic sausage, rye bread, ripe pears or plums, instant coffee loaded with sugar and Carnation Milk, and, of course, some of her famous yellow cake! We, the grandchildren—Elaine, Karen, Laurence, Marvin, Darrell, Gary, and Delvin—salute Edmund and Helen Stebner. We are grateful for this generous couple who believed in us and assisted with our education in very practical ways; moreover, they provided the emotional security, comfort, and safety of a home-away-from-home as we left the isolated nests of our homes in the country to attend the big university in the city.

## RETURN TO THE OLD COUNTRY

Helen and Ed didn't return to the "old country" (as they called it) until about 1962 when they and Ervin flew on a big jet to visit Germany—this time it only took a few hours. Their parents, of course, had passed away, but there was a happy reunion with Helen's older sister and brother in Kandern, West Germany, and a harrowing border crossing to visit her younger sister in East Germany. The German visit also was an opportunity to meet many nieces and nephews.

Ed had been fortunate to have family join him and Helen nearby in Alberta. Two of his brothers immigrated to Alberta a few years after he and Helen had settled in Leduc. Ed's home was a destination for his brothers to stay and become acquainted with their new country and find employment before striking out on their own to eventually settle in the Panoka area. Ed soon had nephews and nieces living in Alberta as well.

Marvin, my brother, and his wife, Lynette, visited Kandern, Germany in 1974. They were met at the train station by Grandma Stebner's nephew and wife. Marvin remembers arriving at the home of Grandma's older sister; he recalls this elderly lady, who resembled ever so much his own grandmother, running down the hill to meet them with tears in her eyes and big hugs and kisses to greet them—her sister's grandchildren she had never met but who were flesh and blood family she loved and cherished at first sight.

## LEGACY

I'm proud of my kinship to the Stebners and Croswells. I'm inspired by their sacrifice and perseverance to rise above difficult circumstances and surroundings and eventually succeed and prosper. Today, my family and I enjoy wonderful blessings because of the legacy of hard work and faith in God handed down to us. My parents and grandparents invested time, energy, and finances in me because they had faith to believe in the potential of my future.

In Hebrews 11, we read at the conclusion of the great Hall of Faith chapter: "*What a record all of these have won by their faith*" (Hebrews 11:39a, GNT). The writer goes on to say in the next chapter:

> As for us, we have this large crowd of witnesses around us. So then, let us rid ourselves of everything that gets in the way, and of the sin which holds on to us so tightly, and let us run with determination the race that lies before us.
>
> —Hebrews 12:1, GNT

I am what I am today, and have accomplished what I have accomplished, because I have been blessed to build on the shoulders of those who have gone before me.

May I in turn leave an example of faith and godly living to the generations who come behind me!

# Chapter Four

# Life on the Farm

Give thanks to the Lord, for he is good;his love en-
dures forever ... For he satisfies the thirsty and fills
the hungry with good things.

—Psalm 107:1, 9

After the war ended in 1945, life on the Balsam Grove farm
slowly began to change. We didn't have the conveniences
of our city cousins, but we didn't know any better. (We were
country mice!) For the most part, we happily accepted our lot
as normal, but we were optimistic that better days lay ahead.
Our parents encouraged us to go to school and get an education. ("So you don't have to 'slave' like we did!")

Our house and farm buildings weren't powered by electricity until I was twelve years old, nor did we have modern
plumbing and running water until I graduated from high
school; we still had an outhouse a short distance down the hill
from our house, complete with last year's Sears and Eaton's
catalogues. We had two wells, but we carried water for household use, drinking and washing from the distant well across the
barnyard—that water was of better quality. As I grew older and

The Leonard and Ella Croswell homestead with new house,
log barn, outbuildings, wood-pile, and nearby haystacks.

stronger, one of my after-school chores was to fetch two pails of water from the faraway well. The nearer well, just a few feet from the house, had been dug to provide for our household needs, but unfortunately the water didn't have a pleasant drinking flavour. Its heavy rust content coloured dishes and clothing reddish-brown. We obtained water for washing clothes in the gas-powered washing machine from a large cattle tank that caught soft rainwater drained off the roof during rainstorms.

The farmhouse was heated with woodstoves (a space heater and a kitchen cookstove) until 1952, when we installed a Booker Self-Feeder Coal Furnace; the furnace was a luxury and kept us warm through the cold winter nights so we didn't have to get up at 1:00 a.m. to replenish the wood. Bedrooms were lit by dim coal-oil lamps; the kitchen and living room were serviced by the hissing, brighter, high-test gas-mantled lamps with built-in air pumps. It wasn't until 1958 that we had the luxury of the electric light bulb.

Laurence and Marvin filled the wood box each evening
to keep the house stoves burning.

We rattled over the dusty back roads in our grey 1949 one-ton Ford truck; when it rained the roads became a soup of muck and gumbo, and the truck would whine its way in low gear along the deep ruts. We didn't own a car until Dad and Mom purchased a new, 1954 Customline Ford. We were proud of our new red-top car, and our family was able to ride to church or town in comfort without anyone having to hold someone on our knees.

Looking back at my childhood days, I realize that our family was emerging from the primitive days of the homestead, and little by little transitioning into the modern era of convenience and mechanization.

## GARDENING

One advantage of living on the farm was that we were almost self-sufficient—we lived mostly off the land. Mom had a large garden which Dad fertilized yearly with stone-boat loads of rotted manure from the barnyard and manure pile. We spent summer days weeding rows and rows of peas, carrots, beans, and summer salad mixtures of lettuce, radishes, and cucumbers. When August arrived, we shelled heaping milk pails of peas, scraped bunches of carrots, and snapped green and yellow beans for Mom to can. Mom had a large steel boiler in which she placed the glass quart sealers filled with vegetables, salt, and water and boiled them; as the jars cooled, the condensing steam would cause the rubber ring to form a seal under the metal lid. The cooled vegetables were then stored on the shelves Dad had built in the basement.

Half of the garden was devoted to potatoes, which were periodically hoed during the long summer days to kill the pernicious pig weeds. As the plants matured, they were mounded with round hills of rich soil. By late July, we dug up new potatoes for immediate eating. New red potatoes, freshly shelled green peas, and young orange carrots oozing with butter were a summer treat! In mid-September, we filled ten to twelve gunny sacks with mature potatoes (red, white, and sometimes yellow fleshed banana) for winter storage in the cool potato bin, located in a corner of the basement. We never lacked for plenty to eat.

## MILKING COWS

Milk cows were vital to the economy of our farm. We milked about ten cows by hand year round. When I was about eight years of age, I learned to sit on a stool beside a cow and squeeze her teats with just the right pressure and rhythm to fill a pail held between my knees with warm, foamy milk. I also learned to duck the swat across my back or head from the cow's swinging tail clearing pestering flies and mosquitoes from her side. Sometimes, however, she would catch me with a stinging swipe when I least expected it!

During the summer, the cows were released to the pasture for grazing. Each night at six o'clock, immediately after supper, we boys were sent to fetch the cows for milking. It seemed they were usually feeding in the farthermost corner of the field. We would take along our collie, Laddie, and when we were near we'd call out, "Co' boss! Co' boss!" Laddie would round up the stragglers, and the cows would form a long line along a worn "cow path," behind the lead cow, Snowball, who had a bell hung around her neck to help us locate the herd should they be hidden in a bluff of trees.

Milking cows was a family time. Every member helped with the milking. While sitting on our stools, we shared and talked about the affairs of the day or what was taking place on the farm. There was often lots of laughter and sometimes for sport (when Dad would let us), we squirted the faces of our yellow farm cats with streams of milk from the cow we were milking; we would laugh as the cat would sputter and gasp but never turn its head away from the fresh jets of warm milk, all the while trying to gulp as much as possible before the stream ceased. The cat would then contentedly wash his face with his two front paws.

One summer I had a pet magpie, Midge, who provided us with humour and amusement during the milking hour. When I was fifteen, I "robbed" a magpie nest of a young bird. Midge was easy to feed—he just opened his mouth, flapped his wings, and squawked whenever we were near. We filled him with table scraps of meat and leftovers. He became a great pet, and after he learned to fly he would land on our heads or shoulders, all the while flapping his wings and squawking for food. If nothing was forthcoming, he would peer and poke his beak into our ears, looking for something he thought might be hidden therein. But

Midge was most entertaining in the barn at milking time. He would tease the cats as they waved their tails and lapped the milk poured into their drinking pan. Midge would hop to the rear of the cats and pull their waving tails. Try as they would, the cats were never fast enough to pounce on Midge, for he quickly flipped above them, squawked in scorn, and continued to tease the cats in a game of "catch me if you can!"

After the cows were milked, portions of fresh milk were measured into pails, and the younger calves housed in the barn were fed. They would greedily suck and snort the warm milk, and the feeder needed to be extra careful not to spill the milk when a calf would deliver a rambunctious bunt. The remaining pails of fresh milk were poured through a clean straining cloth into the large steel bowl at the top of the cream separator. A clean cup was used to dip what was needed from the separator bowl into two-quart sealers and set aside for use in the house. One of my jobs was to turn the handle of the separator that separated the raw milk into two streams of skim milk and rich cream.

The separated milk was very important to our farm operations. The cream was collected in five-gallon cream cans and hung by a rope in the deep open well near the house for cooling; winter ice frozen at the bottom of the well from leaky pails lasted late into the summer. We delivered the cream every week to Newbrook, where it was shipped by train to Palm Dairy in Edmonton; later, when roads were more accessible, a truck came by to pick up the cream. Mom used the cream cheques, sent by mail, to run our household. She purchased supplies and canned goods at the local grocery store; the cheques also provided funds to order from the T. Eaton Catalogue in Winnipeg, Manitoba. Each August we perused the catalogue, filled out the order form, and anticipated the arrival of new shirts, pants, and school supplies to begin the fall school term. How exciting to wait for the train to deliver our parcel from far away Winnipeg.

Some of the cream was also kept aside to churn into butter. This was done by shaking and pounding the creamy liquid on our knees in a two-quart sealer; for larger amounts, cream was poured into a three gallon cream can covered with a white cloth, and then pounded with a wooden forked churning stick until it thickened and suddenly transformed into curds of yellow butter sloshing about in sweet butter milk.

The remaining separated skim milk was mixed with chopped grain and poured into feed troughs for the pigs. The pigs grew fat from their milky feed mixture and were sold to market in Edmonton when they reached two hundred pounds; the pig cheques were used to purchase farm supplies and machinery and to generally keep the farm in operation.

We finally graduated to a milking machine while I was attending high school. Dad also purchased about a dozen Holstein heifers; when they "freshened" with new calves, our milk production greatly increased and augmented our farm operations.

## BERRY PICKING

Fall was berry picking time. Some of the old brush heaps left over from clearing the land were still piled and rotting along the edges of fields and produced a quantity of red raspberries. Many times it would be necessary to gingerly make our way to the berry bushes by stepping over and around dead tree stumps and branches, often guarded by a healthy growth of nettles and thorns to scrape or sting our skin. But once the luscious fruit was harvested, the red berries made delicious deserts, whether fresh with sugar and cream, or canned in quart sealers to be stored for a cold winter's day.

Blueberry picking became a major campaign. Come August, Mom would partner with neighbours and travel in a cavalcade. We loaded pails and lunches into our grey one-ton truck and rumbled and bounced along the rough dirt road toward a location near Long Lake that had once been burned over but had since re-grown with brush and low-bush blueberries. One year, the hills literally were coloured blue with berries. Believe it or not, that fall, when Darrell was still a toddler and needed to be carried to the blueberry patches, Mom, Marvin, and I picked seventeen water pails of blue berries! When the berries were transported home, our family worked as a team to clean the berries, spreading the berries on large platters and separating green berries and particles of brush and bushes from the ripe blue fruit, all the while popping fresh berries into our blue mouths as we worked. We had blueberry pies, blueberry jam, and quarts and quarts of canned blueberries all neatly stored in sealers like blue sentinels guarding the cold storage shelves of our basement.

Another addition to our fresh fruit diet was the Saskatoon berry. Saskatoons ripened profusely on willow-like bushes along the eastern border of our farm during the month of August. They were easy to pick, and we would quickly filled our berry pails with these dark purple berries and bring them home to clean. They were either eaten fresh with sugar and cream, or became filling for Mom's homemade pies. Saskatoons are sweet with a unique flavour, and they're a special treat enjoyed by many western Canadians.

There were other berries growing wild as well: strawberries, high bush cranberries, low bush cranberries, and choke cherries. Each fall Mom added sugar and gelatine to the berries and boiled them into delicious jams and jellies to spread on toast during the long cold winter.

## BUTCHERING MEAT

Each fall when the weather turned cold and heavy frost appeared on the morning grass, Dad, Uncle Bill Trenholm (Dad's brother-in-law), and Uncle Walter lent a helping hand to butcher a beef, usually a young steer. I never liked to be near the killing of the animal, for Uncle Bill usually shot the animal with a 22-rifle or knocked it out with an axe, and Uncle Walter cut its throat so it would bleed and drain as much blood as possible. The animal was hung head down by the hind legs for skinning and removal of the innards. The naked carcass was often left hanging overnight for stretching before being carved the next day into steaks and roasts.

The butchering of the pork was a bit more involved. A fire was kindled outside to boil water in a steel barrel; the dead pig was doused repeatedly in the hot water, head first, while the three men vigorously scraped the bristly hair from the pig's skin. Like the beef, the pork carcass was hung and the innards removed. The liver and heart were saved to be coated with flour and fried, often with onions, usually the evening after the butchering. Some of our neighbours boiled and removed eatable portions of the animal's head to make head-cheese. Many enjoyed the delicacy, but Mom was too squeamish about the process and could never bring herself to make such a recipe. The main carcass was carved into various cuts of bacon, chops, side-ribs, and roasts. Until we got electricity, it was stored in a cold, safe granary where it would freeze for safe keeping, or mom would can portions in glass quart sealers and store them on her basement shelves. Like I said, we were never hungry, for we were nearly self-sufficient!

## THE CHICKEN COOP

We also had a chicken coop situated not far from the house. Each spring we would order a hundred chicks from an Edmonton hatchery. The little chicks were temporarily kept in the house until they learned to eat chick starter crumbles and drink from the sealer water founts; soon they were moved to a small chick house heated by a warming stove with a circular tin cover until they sprouted feathers and were housed in the chicken coop. The young pullets would begin to lay eggs, and when they were in full production we sold crates of eggs that were picked up by train or truck in Newbrook and shipped to Edmonton.

One day when I was about three years old, I entered the chicken coop to watch the hens scratch in the clean straw. I was fascinated by their behaviour and scurrying about. For some unknown reason, except maybe childish fun, I climbed up to where the egg nests had been built, reached into a nest, picked up an egg, and threw it onto the floor. It created a scurry of activity as the hens quickly gathered round to gobble up the broken egg. I was so intrigued by their frenzied behaviour that I laughed with glee and continued from nest to nest throwing eggs to the floor and watching the hens quickly scamper to eat them. This went on for a couple of days. I thought it great fun, and Mom couldn't understand why the egg count had gone down so abruptly and significantly—that is, until one day when I was caught (I think by Grandpa Croswell), and my laughter turned to tears as Mom applied her black strap of correction. The egg count returned to normal the next day.

We also ordered a few roosters among the spring chickens. Come fall, when the roosters were full grown, Dad and Mom designated a day for butchering roosters. A big boiler of hot water was heated on the cook stove, and Dad sharpened his axe

Three Generations: Grandpa Fred Croswell sits on the bailer to watch over his son, Leonard, and grandsons, Marvin, Darrell, and Laurence.

and set up a big chopping block. The squawking roosters were captured the night before when they couldn't see to escape, and then placed in a large chicken crate. The next morning, their heads were dully severed on the block, and the headless bodies thrown aside to kick and flop until they were quiet enough for us to catch them and douse them in boiling water. This was a family affair, and each of us would clean a bird by pulling the steaming, wet feathers from the fowl assigned to us. Dad and Mom usually cleaned the innards from each bird, being very careful not to cut the crop but save the gizzards and heart, which were special delicacies. Mom would then fry one of the roosters in fresh farm cream. Served with new potatoes, it was a delicacy not to be forgotten!

## BREAKFAST

One of the most important meals at our house was breakfast. It was a nutritious start to the day, and we ate it around 7:30 each morning after the milking in the barn was completed. Breakfast began with bowls of hot Quaker Rolled Oats or Sunny Boy Cereal (a mixture of whole wheat, flax, and rye), which Mom cooked on the wood stove. Sugar was spooned liberally over the steaming porridge, and milk and cream poured generously around the outer edge. After the porridge was served, fried eggs on a platter were passed along accompanied with thick slices of homemade bread toasted on a wire mesh placed on the wood cook stove. The toast was slathered with home churned butter until dripping and spread with homemade jam or honey. Each person prepared their own cup of hot chocolate, stirring a smooth mixture of cocoa, sugar, and cream to which was added hot scalding water. We left the table full and ready for any giants we might face!

## SOWING AND REAPING

When Leonard and Walter began clearing the homestead of trees and brush, they mainly used axes and teams of horses. But as time went on, they began to accumulate "modern" farm machinery. The brothers purchased a tractor with steel wheels and lugs. It took a strong man to turn the steering wheel of the clumsy iron machine, but it had power and traction to easily out-pull horses on the breaking plow as it rumbled over the newly brushed fields; there was also power to yank out stubborn stumps and boulders still imbedded in the gray-wooded soil. Fields were disc-harrowed, and hay was cut with horse machinery. By the end of the 1940s, a Model D John Deere tractor with rubber wheels was purchased to more easily pull larger machinery over the cleared land as well as provide power to turn the pulley on the giant threshing machine.

The sights, sounds, and smells of harvest days made fall a special season of the year. There was a sense of urgency, since by late August the long summer days of Alberta began to significantly shorten, and killing frosts were not uncommon. By the time I was nine, I was recruited to drive one of the two John Deere AR tractors Leonard and Walter had recently purchased. Uncle Walter and I were a team: he rode and operated the grain binder, and I drove the tractor. We were assigned the McCormick horse binder; moving gears were driven by the large drive wheel, which meant that when the wheel was not turning, nothing on the binder would perform its duty. Since I was still too young to be driving a tractor in a grain field, pulling a fully operating binder with sharp grain-cutting blades, moving pulleys and reels, and a knotter that tied the grain into bundles and kicked them onto the bundle carrier, Uncle Walter tied a long rope to the John Deere's stick clutch so he could stop tractor and binder at any time should there be an emergency. I was proud when he told other grownups that he never used the rope once. I stopped every time he called out, "Whoa!" and we kept up to my dad and Grandpa Croswell with their tractor and new live-power-take-off John Deere binder.

After the binder dropped the bundles in bunches on the stubble field, the next task was to stook the sheaves by hand into neat pyramids with the heads of grain pointing to the sun so the grain could easily dry and be ready for the threshing crew. By mid-to-late September, most of the grain fields were cut and stooked, and some of the early-cut grain was ready for threshing. What a thrill to see the John Deere Model D pulling the big Waterloo threshing machine into the first field for levelling and set up. All the belts were fitted on the correct pulleys, and the large straw blower turned in the direction of the blowing wind. We usually had three pick-up racks, each drawn by a team of horses (later by tractors). Dad, Uncle Bill Trenholm, and Bill Fedun would lead their teams around the field and skilfully build their load of bundles on the racks to be pitch-forked into the hungry mouth of the threshing machine. Uncle Walter was in charge of the general management of the threshing machine; he helped pitch bundles, shovel back weed seeds, look after greasing the machine's numerous pulleys and moving shakers, stop and start the tractor when necessary, and endeavour to keep operations running smoothly and efficiently. The straw would blow into an ever rising straw-stack, and the wheat, barley, or oats would pour down the spout into the granary. Often I was assigned to the dusty granary to shovel back the golden grain and keep the long spout clear of the rising heap of grain in the bin. I would also join the men for the four o'clock lunch of hot tea and coffee, sweet Cool-Aide, salmon sandwiches, and fresh baking, which might be deep-fried donuts, oatmeal cookies, or chocolate cake. How we looked for Mom's grey ton-truck to come bouncing onto the field, for we knew it was the sign lunch had arrived!

Each evening, after darkness settled on the crisp fall evenings, the moon would shine brightly on the old log barn, and we would hear the rattle of Uncle Bill's wagon, the snorting of his horses, and the music of his shrill vibrato whistle. We knew that threshing was finished for the day. The horses were tied to the rail fence and fed oat bundles, and the men would walk into the house and wash up for supper. Soon the threshers gathered around the kitchen table for Mom's meal of roast beef and gravy or cream-fried chicken, creamy mashed potatoes, salads, beet and dill pickles, and, of course, homemade pie (blueberry, Saskatoon, or apple) loaded with heaps of whipped cream. It was all complemented with steaming cups of hot tea or coffee. The hearty laughter of the threshers, their good-natured banter, and the hissing of the mantled gas lamps are sounds of harvest days that still linger in my memory.

## SCHOOL DAYS

Monday, September 4, 1950. I was six years old and ready to begin my first day of formal education at the one-roomed Balsam Grove School located one mile from our house. Mom had prepared me for grade one the year before, and I could fluently read *Fun with Dick and Jane* and was well acquainted with the family of Dick, Jane, Baby, Mother, Father, and pets, Puff and Spot. I would crawl into my high chair and read to family and visitors the words and phrases that were repeated over and over. "Jump, Spot, jump! Look, Dick, look!" Mom's only regret about her teaching pedagogy was that she taught me to point a finger at each word I read, so my teacher had to wean me of that habit. Mom drove me on the first day of school in the ton truck. I remember being frightened, and one of the grade eight boys, Pat Robinson, picked me up in his arms to welcome me. There were about eighteen students that year from grade one to eight, and the teacher, Mrs. Victoria Croswell, assigned me to a double desk beside the only other grade one student, Myrna Kent.

There were advantages to attending a one-roomed school. One of them was hearing stories the other grades read from their readers during oral reading. I was an avid listener to all the adventures. Best of all, each day after lunch, "Teacher," as we called Victoria, read a chapter to the class from one of the books someone had brought to school or was supplied by the Thorhild County School Division. We read the exciting detective adventures of the Hardy boys, Joe and Frank, or classics like *Robin Hood* and *Little Women*. I was so intrigued listening to the Thornton W. Burgess series of Peter Rabbit and his friends at the Laughing Pool and Green Meadows that I requested individual books for birthday or Christmas presents, or saved up money myself and ordered them from Eaton's catalogue.

Fall turned to winter, and since I walked the one mile to school, my mother made certain that I "did not freeze like she did" when she walked to Newbrook School as a little girl. She studied the catalogue with me and ordered a big parka with a fur-trimmed hood and wrapped me with a scarf to keep my nose warm. My outfit was completed with outer leather mitts fitted with inner knitted mittens (knitted by Grandma Croswell), and my feet were snug in felt boots. I was ready for any Arctic weather that might be hurled against me. And believe me, sometimes cold blizzards settled in and you needed Mom's winter clothes to stay warm! The roads would blow in, and we were able to walk much of the distance to school on hardened snowdrifts. When the county snow plow cleared the country road, we climbed the towering banks and walked on the snow piled high by the plows.

During the frigid winter, Fridays at Balsam Grove School were designated special lunch days. Each student brought a potluck ingredient for the home-made soup that simmered on the wood and coal stove at the back of the room: rice, barley, carrots, potatoes, turnips, or perhaps a sealer of canned meat from someone's home cellar. The aroma wafting through the small school room was a pleasant motivation to finish arithmetic and reading lessons. No one ever knew for certain what that soup would taste like, but with added salt and pepper, it was always a delicious addition to our cold baloney, egg, or peanut butter sandwiches. Mom had purchased a lunch pail for me, complete with thermos bottle for hot cocoa, but the thermos only lasted until I kicked at a senior student who caught my leg and I fell backwards and broke the glass lining. The hot soup was a happy substitute during the cold winter months.

The year 1952 saw a large increase in attendance at the school as the first baby boomers began to attend. The grade one class swelled to six as Geraldine, Sharon, Patsy, Arnid, Marvin, and Reggie formed an entire row on the right hand side of the little classroom, and Teacher was required to spend more time assisting the new beginners who represented differing scholastic abilities but were all in grade one. The challenge for Victoria Croswell was that she had eight grades to teach, and the additional challenge to give appropriate attention to each grade became daunting. Balsam Grove was not the only school with increased enrolment. The war had been over for seven years, and many babies were born throughout the school districts of the county.

The next year, Thorhild County followed the example of most school boards in Alberta and began to consolidate one-roomed schools into new large centralized schools located in the small hamlets and towns of the region. Classes were now organized by grades. We rode to Newbrook School on Mr. Bereziuk's yellow school bus. Every school day he stopped his bus at the "church corner," a half mile north of our house, where about a dozen students met to catch the bus. What a formidable task for Mr. Bereziuk to navigate over the side roads, many of which were not yet gravelled and turned into greasy gumbo after a rain storm! During winter months, blowing snow was another daunting challenge, and Mr. Bereziuk would drive his bus headlong into a drift, snow flying over the hood, hoping to make it safely to the other side. At times, however, the bus would become hopelessly stuck in a mound of deep snow. Student riders were called upon to help push the bus out of the snow. Sad to say, but at least once older students deliberately pushed the bus further into the ditch to miss attending school.

Thankfully, Tommy Brooks had a tractor and yanked the yellow bus out of the ditch and drift. We made it to school, but were happily late that morning for classes.

I was frightened to begin attending the school at Newbrook, Not only would there be many students I'd never met, but the teacher assigned to my grade four class was Mrs. Nuttycombe, and she had a reputation for being very strict. She was given a challenge, of course, to teach a room full of new students who came from various one-roomed schools in a fifteen mile radius from such diverse communities as Darling, Weasel Creek, Birchfield, Alpen, Abee, Balsam Grove, and Newbrook. Most of these students had never met each other, so there was a getting-to-know-you and adjustment period to attending the larger school. Suffice it to say, there was no "fooling around" in Mrs. Nuttycombe's class, for she ran a tight ship. One of our highlights that year was a play performed in the Newbrook Community Hall and the County Festival. I played the King of Hearts. A volunteer from the Newbrook Ladies Aid Club sewed a special white suit from flour sacks covered with red hearts for me to wear. I was embarrassed about wearing such a ludicrous costume, but I did it for Mrs. Nuttycombe, and she was pleased!

## BABY BROTHER

Another highlight during grade four was the birth of a second brother, Darrell, on May 5, 1954. He was to be Mom and Dad's girl, but his black hair and features told us he was all boy! We thought he was the cutest baby we'd ever seen. Dad was older and mellower and was not in such a hurry to get things done. He loved baby Darrell and took time from his hectic pace of chores and work in the fields to play with him and cuddle him. It seemed that if Dad disciplined Marvin and me for whatever reason, Darrell escaped!

Soon the school year passed and we were promoted to grade five. The new teacher was Miss Melnyk, a first year teacher from "Normal School." She had a happy disposition and progressive ideas about teaching. I loved Miss Melnyk and did whatever I could to please her. It was one of my happiest years in school.

## NEIGHBOUR COUSINS

The Balsam Grove community during my growing up years was still populated by eight families with Croswell roots. Uncle Walter's family (Sharon, Wayne, Dennis, Bonnie, and Maureen), who lived only a quarter mile to the south, were more than cousins—they were almost brothers and sisters. We walked to school together, played games together, discussed life together, and yes, at times like normal siblings, squabbled together. We even designed and built our own playground in the woods between our homes, complete with tree club-house. We hung an old cowbell in a tree so we could summon each other when it was play time. One ride I invented nearly ended in tragedy. I tied a pulley to the top of a tree and installed a homespun rope I'd poorly woven from binder twine. I tied the end to a pail and proceeded to show everyone how we could pull the pail from the ground to the tree top. It would be a great look out! But disaster nearly occurred when we decided to pull my four year old brother, Darrell, to the top of the tree on a trial run. When the bucket neared the top, the binder twine rope unravelled and Darrell came crashing to the ground. I was horrified to think that Darrell might be seriously injured. Thankfully he was okay, but he'd never volunteer to be a look-out for our party again—nor would anyone else! It really put a damper on our enthusiasm for the playground.

## SUMMER HOLIDAYS

Summer on the farm was filled with fun and mixed with the drudgery of necessary chores. School was out, and during the long sunny days we ran about the yard and fields in bare feet.

Our play was often imaginative and creative. We built a model community and a miniature play farm, serviced by roads and a town with stores and a garage. Since there were no Lego blocks or Fisher Price villages, the buildings were constructed from wooden scraps scrounged from Dad's junk pile. Road building equipment made from empty Prem cans became bulldozers that excavated and scraped out ditches and formed the road beds. Sand gravelled the roads, and used oil was sprinkled on the surfaces to form pavement. A few toy trucks and cars received at Christmas (Tonkas were unheard of) made everything seem real to our minds, and we sped along our infrastructure of highways and side roads to various make-believe appointments and assignments.

Everyone was assigned chores on a mixed farm. As soon as we were able, we gathered eggs from the hen house, cleaned and bedded the calves' stalls in the barn, rounded up cows each evening for milking, and learned to milk a cow almost as soon as we could hold a pail between our legs.

July was haying season. We worked in the hay field helping Dad harvest the sweet smelling broom grass and clover. Dad pitched the dried hay, which had been raked into neat mounds, into an ingenious home-made contraption called a hay boat. The hay boat was a rectangular frame of rails pulled along the ground by a tractor. As Dad pitched hay into the empty boat, we boys jumped and stomped to press and pack the hay into the corners until Dad had a well-formed hay stack that would shed rain. The completed stacks were pulled along the ground to their final destination near the barnyard. The back gate of the boat was undone while the flat front railing was staked to the ground; the rails were pulled out from underneath, leaving a neat stack intact. The front and back rail forms were replaced, and we were ready to start all over again. This haying activity lasted until Dad purchased a hay-baler, and jumping in the hay was replaced by lifting and lugging heavy bales and storing them in hot, dusty sheds—it was back-breaking, no-fun summer work.

## SUMMER HOLIDAYS AT THE STEBNERS

One of our summer highlights was an annual holiday with Grandma and Grandpa Stebner and Uncle Ralph on their farm at Dorenlee. It was a fun place to stay for one week, and Marvin and I looked forward to the holiday. Grandma had only one recipe for cake—a yellow, moist cake with thick, creamy icing. Mmmm, it was so good! And she always stored a variety of multi-coloured soft drinks in her cupboard for us kids: 7-Up, Orange Crush, Grape Crush, and Canada Dry. In her large black purse were Jersey Milk chocolate bars! Often during the week we'd speed with Uncle Ralph in the Stebners' half-ton Ford down the long dusty laneway, turn right onto the gravel highway, turn right again at the top of the hill, and coast down the steep slope that led to Dorenlee's lone general store and two tall grain elevators. We purchased the few groceries Grandma had ordered, and as a treat, Uncle Ralph bought a fresh pop for seven cents from the store cooler. At other times we drove the twenty miles to Bashaw to purchase supplies and buy a large slice of orange cheese from the Bashaw Dairy.

The Stebners lived beside the railroad track. When we heard the big freight trains in the distance puffing along the track, we scampered up the wooden stairs to peer out the end window and watch the train rattle by in the cut bank below

Grandma's garden. We gawked with fascination as the freight cars and their cargos jerked and creaked behind the huge steam locomotives, and there was always a red caboose dangling on the end with a conductor perched precariously in his roof-top cupola overlooking the entire line of cars. Sometimes we had time to rush across the garden to peer over the cliff's bank, and the engineer or caboose conductor would notice us and wave a friendly greeting.

Grandma always raised a dozen or so geese and ducks. They swam about with their goslings and ducklings in a muddy slough just below the barnyard. One day, I decided to wade in the water with the birds in my bare feet. It was a foolish decision, for I stepped on the head of a rusty nail stuck in a piece of rotting board hidden in the muddy waters. The pain was excruciating, and the nail's head became trapped behind the skin of my foot. I was unable to remove the head through the hole in my skin, and when I lifted my foot from the water, the board was dangling below. I began to scream at the top of my voice until Grandma came running from the house and down the hill to rescue me. She dislodged the nail and led me to the farm house where she bathed the pierced foot and covered it with a Band-Aid. When I returned home, the wound appeared to be healing while I limped about the farm yard for a couple of weeks. That should have been the end of the story, but one day I felt an itching on the side of my leg and noted a yellow streak running up a vein. Mom knew exactly what it was.

"Blood poisoning!" she gasped. Mom realized this was an emergency. Since we lived in the back woods at Newbrook and were miles away from a doctor in Radway, I sat in a chair while Mom proceeded to lance the infected foot with a large darning needle. She carefully squeezed and cleaned out the infection, washing the wound and filling the hole with Lysol. I screamed for dear life! Mom apologized over and over for the pain she was causing, but thoroughly cleansed the wound and the infection did not return. "Dr. Ella" had experience with kids stepping on nails with bare feet.

## SPIRITUAL ROOTS, TRAINING, AND GROWTH

Each day, the after-breakfast ritual around the table included a short Bible reading, after which our family would kneel by our chairs, Mom or a guest would pray, and everyone recited the Lord's Prayer. Each evening before bedtime, we children knelt beside our beds and prayed the child's prayer: "Now I lay me down to sleep, I pray the Lord my soul to keep. If I should die before I wake, I pray the Lord my soul to take." At the end of the prayer we added a "God bless" family and friends we thought needed to be remembered in our prayer. On Sunday afternoons, we attended the little white Standard Church one half mile to the north of our red, brick-siding farmhouse. During my pre-school years, the Reverend Norman and Laura Wiggins and their family of girls were our pastors. Sunday attendance had declined from the revival days to about twenty-five or thirty people. Attendance dwindled even further as people moved to the city, died, or simply lost interest. The Wiggins moved to Edmonton to pastor the Edmonton Standard Church.

A young woman, Mildred Shouldice, was appointed pastor of the Balsam Grove Standard Church. She was a graduate of Prairie Bible College in Three Hills, Alberta, and was an excellent preacher. But attendance didn't increase. However, one Sunday afternoon, Miss Shouldice preached and gave an invitation for anyone to come forward to trust Jesus as Lord. I became greatly disturbed that I was not right with God, and as the small congregation sang an invitation hymn, I hung on to the seat in front of me to keep from going forward for prayer. I

Miss Shouldice provided music lessons on the piano
accordion for two homesteaders' sons.

blinked back tears and, with face in hands, knelt at my seat for
the closing prayer. Miss Shouldice, recognizing the Holy Spirit was dealing with my heart, came over and prayed with me. It
was my first encounter with God speaking intensely about my
relationship with Him.

Miss Shouldice was gifted musically. She could sing, play
the guitar, and had received piano lessons as a girl in Calgary.
Mom and Dad recognized that I was musically inclined and
made arrangements with Miss Shouldice to teach music lessons to Marvin and me on the piano accordion. Miss Shouldice would be paid with spare cash and farm produce: eggs,
milk, cream, and sealers of fruit. We ordered a new 48 Bass
Frontalini accordion from the Eaton's catalogue, and soon
Marvin and I were practicing music scales and simple songs
on our new accordion.

Most of our lessons involved using the right hand, since
Miss Shouldice hadn't received lessons on the accordion but
rather the piano. I learned to match the bass chords on my left

hand "by ear" while playing the melody on the right hand "by note," just as Miss Shouldice did. Nevertheless, I learned the basics of notation and musical timing. Marvin was also musically inclined and had a beautiful singing voice, but practicing scales on the accordion was not for him. After coaxing, threatening, and cajoling by Mom, Marvin finally dropped out of accordion lessons. I don't think he even remembered where to find middle C! But I continued on. It was a major benefit to my spiritual growth, since I used a hymn book for many of the songs I practiced and I learned to play and sing many of the old hymns of the church.

Our entertainment on cold winter Saturday evenings was often a family hymn sing. Dad had previously purchased a used guitar for five dollars and knew about six chords. He strummed with a thumb pick and was skilled enough to chord along with our hymns and gospel songs. Mom had a strong lead voice, Dad sang bass, and Marvin and I learned to sing parts and harmonize. We weren't confident enough to sing publically, nor did anyone ask us to. Humorously, Dad often compared us to the musical Dafoe family who attended the Newbrook Pentecostal Church and would say, "If only the Dafoes could hear us!" The family sings instilled in me a love for music and singing as well as filled my mind with spiritual tunes and words. I learned to play Dad's few chords on the guitar and ordered a *Learn How to Play the Guitar* book from the catalogue and expanded my playing ability. I gradually replaced Dad as our family accompanist, and I kept on singing.

The little white Standard Church at Balsam Grove nearly closed during the mid to late 1950s with perhaps a dozen or fewer people attending. Mom and Dad decided to attend the Pentecostal Church in Newbrook, which had a congregation of about sixty people who worshipped on Sunday mornings. The services were orderly and well planned by the pastor, the

Reverend White. Mom and Dad made friends with a number of the Newbrook church attendees and joined some of them at times after church for dinners in their homes.

I developed a friendship with Elder Sloboda, who was one year older than I. His family attended the Newbrook church, and we both attended Newbrook High School, so we had much in common. Elder and I became teenage friends and spent Sunday afternoons together after church, either at his home or my home. We often romped about the farms with our 22-calibre rifles, but shot very little. We mostly roamed the back hills and woods together. At other times we played board games, and we became "crack shots" at aiming and flicking an opponent's crokinole discs off the playing board. We also formed a trio with Marvin and sang at church and school variety nights.

Newbrook school teacher, Fred Revega, was the youth leader of Christ's Ambassadors, and I was able to attend some of the CA meetings and socials the church families hosted. I recall sledding and tobogganing down the steep hill slopes at the Ralph Johnson ranch in White Mud. I'm grateful for those days of spiritual formation during my high school years, and for leaders like Mr. Revega, who cared enough to invest in my spiritual growth.

One other spiritual influence remained constant from my early childhood to my later teen years: Newbrook Camp Meeting. Every summer, shortly after the July long weekend, a large white gospel tent was pitched on a grassy clearing among a cool bluff of trembling aspens near the Balsam Grove Standard Church. The enclosed canvas meeting place was scattered with clean wheat straw; wooden benches were installed facing a low framed platform that served both as kneeling altar and raised stage for the preaching pulpit. Each evening, hissing gas lanterns were hung on pegs that jutted from the centre tent

Daily Vacation Bible School was held each July in the gospel tent pitched on the Standard Church camp grounds. Can you identify Marvin in the second row and Laurence in the third?

poles to provide light for the congregational singing and the reading of Scriptures. People drove in from miles around and set up housekeeping in the little white cottages built around the edge of the grounds, or camped in tents pitched for the entire ten day retreat.

As in the 1930s, the preaching was strongly animated, and the congregation punctuated the preaching with hearty rounds of "Amen!" "Hallelujah!" or "Praise the Lord!" Guest singers from neighbouring Amber Valley often came with guitars and their own brand of gospel music. Each day, a Daily Vacation Bible School was held with special prizes and awards for children who learned their verses and had perfect attendance. There were many crafts for the children during the week, but there was one activity I will always remember: painting the plaster-of-paris plaques Grace Brooks made from her rubbery moulds. After drying, painting, and shellacking, the scenes and mottos looked quite professional—actually store bought!

## LEGACY

My family provided me with a legacy of faith from childhood until my teenage years. Paul wrote to the young man, Timothy: *"I am reminded of your sincere faith, which first lived in your grandmother Lois, and in your mother Eunice and, I am persuaded, now lives in you also"* (2 Timothy 1:5). How important for parents to surround their children with godly examples and provide opportunities for worship and fellowship! Grandparents reinforce this faith and provide models for their grandchildren to follow. In the book of Exodus, God says "[He shows] *love to a thousand generations of those who love* [Him] *and keep His commandments* (Exodus 20:5–6).

God began a work of faith in my grandparents and parents. I am passing this legacy of faith to the generations of grandchildren and great grandchildren that follow me.

# Chapter Five

# Fork in the Road

Therefore, if anyone is in Christ
he is a new creation;
the old has gone away; the new has come!
—2 Corinthians 5:17

My parents, especially Mom, became disgruntled with life on the farm without hydro. Many of the communities to the north and south had been serviced by Calgary Power, but Balsam Grove had been overlooked. After much discussion and planning, Mom and Dad decided to purchase a house in Edmonton, and in the spring of 1957, they temporarily moved to the city anticipating a better life style. They moved into a large two-storey house on the south side, and Mom cooked for a couple of boarders while Dad worked on construction sites building new houses. The farm was not sold, and Dad seeded the land in the spring to take off a crop in the fall.

I didn't immediately move to Edmonton with our family, but instead stayed behind in the village of Newbrook to complete my remaining two months of grade seven. I was fortunate to live with Uncle Charlie, Dad's youngest brother, and his wife, Aunt Else; they had two young children, Dale and Darlene. I thoroughly enjoyed my stay with Uncle Charlie and Aunt Else, for they were young at heart and a great deal of fun. Every day after school I looked after Darlene, their cute toddler daughter and my cousin. This often involved transporting her about town to visit school friends at Megley's Garage; the baby sitting freed Aunt Else to serve customers and care for the books at the Esso bulk oil franchise, while Uncle Charlie managed the gravel trucks and carting business. Uncle Charlie knew what would make a thirteen year-old boy happy, so he purchased a flat-roofed, start-by-crank Chevrolet (about 1929 model) for $25, which he allowed me to drive along the back road and across the railway tracks to milk the cow each evening at his nearby farm. It was a busy household. Uncle Charlie and Aunt Else made me feel part of their work, and I felt important riding down the main street of Newbrook in the big red cab-over gravel truck—proud to be part of such an up-and-coming enterprise.

But Edmonton did not make Dad happy. Working in the city was not for him. He'd never really worked for an employer before, and he longed for the animals and open fields of the farm. So when Calgary Power promised to provide electricity to the farms of Balsam Grove District, Dad and Mom decided to move back to the old homestead with the promise of new electrical conveniences. Vincent, one of Mom's boarders, wired the old house and strung insulated cable to the barns and well. Hydro poles were placed along the country road, and later that summer my family returned from the city to the old homestead farm—excitedly anticipating the Calgary Power hook-up.

Mom and Dad were gracious in consideration of promises they'd made to me about schooling in Edmonton, and arranged for me to live with Grandma and Grandpa Stebner during the month of September to attend grade eight classes at Queen Alexandra Junior High School; it was mainly a face saving recess, since I'd expected to be living in Edmonton by September and had announced to my teachers that I would be transferring schools. However, the month at Queen Alex was an experience I thoroughly enjoyed, and my competitive temperament rose to the challenge of the high level of academic expectations held by the teachers. I regretted not being able to continue; nevertheless, I returned in October and re-enrolled at Newbrook School, a motivated student, "showing-off" my notes, and wishing to excel in my grades.

Electricity was soon connected to our farm house, and for the first time we were able to turn on a light with the flick of a switch. I remember gazing at the glowing bulb in our living room without hearing the hiss of a gas lamp hanging from a ceiling hook. There were other advantages, too. We could plug in various electrical appliances, including a radio and a new black and white television. It wasn't long until we bought an electric milking machine, which revolutionized our farming.

I also got an electric radio for my upstairs attic room, so I could listen to Elvis Presley and Buddy Holly. I ordered an electric guitar and amplifier from the Eaton's catalogue, and soon I was strumming bar chords to accompany the top forty rock 'n' roll hits CJCA played twenty-four-seven over the airwaves. I'd previously sung gospel and country-western songs, but soon Hit Parade numbers like "Don't Be Cruel" and "All Shook Up" began to enter my repertoire as well.

## HIGH SCHOOL DAYS

When I entered high school, I continued my singing and guitar playing. A popular country music show was aired live each Saturday on CHED radio station in Edmonton. I was about sixteen years old when I gathered up enough courage to audition for the show. Walking down the stairs to CHED studios on Jasper Avenue was intimidating for a country boy from the back woods, but when I sang, the musicians and radio technicians stood around the studio speakers and appeared pleased with what they heard. I passed the audition and sang on the radio show with full musical back-up: fiddle, guitars, stand-up bass, and vocals. The songs chosen for me to sing were interesting. The first, "Burning Bridges Behind Me," was a country song on the popular hit parade, but the second, to my surprise, was "Just a Closer Walk with Thee," and I was featured with vocal background voices on the spiritual segment of the show. I dedicated it to my Grandmother Croswell, who had taught me as a pre-schooler to love music and singing.

Despite the fact that I loved singing and had my first thrill of public performance, I wasn't prepared to give up my education to pursue a music career. I knew the music business was too risky to abandon the security of an education; furthermore, I couldn't make the contacts necessary to continue from Newbrook.

At the time that I passed Alberta's grade nine departmental exams and graduated to grade ten, Newbrook High was a very small school. There were only ten students in grade ten, but I was blessed and fortunate to have two of the very best teachers I could ever have hoped for to start my high school journey. My home room teacher, who taught all the basics (Math, English, and Science), was Miss Madeline White, the daughter of the Pentecostal Minister whose church was next door to the school. The other was Mr. Eugene Malo, who taught French and Physical Education. Both were first year teachers who made education and learning fun. Moreover, they taught our class the value of discipline and good study habits, and they encouraged us to always do our best. Grade ten provided a firm foundation to carry me through the remaining two years of high school studies.

My grade ten marks were excellent, but in grade eleven I faltered. It's not that I didn't pass all my courses, but my marks were just not in the honours range. Fortunately, the grades were still good enough to qualify me for enrolment in six grade-twelve departmental courses, which were needed to graduate with senior matriculation and permit enrolment at the University of Alberta.

## ROCK 'N' ROLL

In the summer after grade ten, my cousin, Diana Croswell, who was a friend and fan of my music, set up an audition for me with Edmonton's popular rock band, Wes Dekus and the Club 93 Rebels. I'd written some songs and we wondered if Wes Dekus might be interested in recording any of them. He listened and expressed interest. Wes Dekus began setting up practice sessions for me with his band at the studio of CJCA; Mom and Dad graciously drove me to Edmonton at various times through the fall and winter, sometimes on precariously snowy roads, so I could practice singing with the Rebels and record a song at the studio.

During the winter of 1960–61, I recorded "I Forgot to Remember to Forget" with the Rebels and The Shamrocks, a popular male group in Edmonton, as background voices. It was a good recording and was played on the radio; however, it didn't have the catchy-edge needed to become a profitable seller on the market. I sang the song with the Rebels at their Big Band Spectacular on Easter Monday, April 3, 1961, in Edmonton's Jubilee Auditorium. What a thrill to sing with the band in that beautiful auditorium with spectacular acoustics

Laurence became a "pop" singer during his teens with
a song on the CJCA radio hit parade.

and lighting and a large audience, including my mother and Diana, to applaud my performance!

A few months after recording, I learned that the band members who played for the Rebels decided to form their own band, the Nomads, without Wes Dekus as leader. Since I'd previously recorded with these musicians, I inquired if they might be interested in recording a couple of new songs—this time songs I'd written. They listened to the songs and agreed. We booked the CJCA studio and recorded an unusual song I'd dreamed up from reading the *Free Press Weekly* about a "Pen Pal Girl" who lived in Australia. It was all fiction, of course, and was before the days of Internet. We also recorded a second song, "Stranded," which I also had written. An unknown company, Stardust Records, in Barrie, Ontario pressed some

45 rpm records, and by the fall of 1962, I was ready to release the recording to radio CJCA.

## UNIVERSITY DAYS

I eventually graduated from high school with my senior matriculation and was accepted at the University of Alberta into the faculty of Education. Ever since grade ten I'd felt my gifting was teaching. When Miss White would assign various teaching assignments for each student to instruct the class, I'd say to myself, "This is for me!" I believed I could be a successful teacher, and set my goal to graduate with a Bachelor of Education. My parents were delighted. I would not have to "slave like they did!"

That summer, after I was accepted at the U of A, I helped Dad on the farm until late July, when I learned that Standard Gravel, a large construction company, was building a bi-pass road around Newbrook and were looking for help. Uncle Charlie hauled gravel for the company and put in a good word for me with the site superintendent. I was hired by Standard Gravel with the prestigious job title of bull cook! I peeled potatoes, cut meat, washed dishes, cleaned sinks, mopped the men's bunkhouse floors, and generally assisted the cooks in any way I could. It was a happy summer, for I got along wonderfully with the cooks and workers during the next two months. Moreover, it set me up for a job the following summer on the survey crew with Standard Gravel.

## ON THE HIT PARADE

I moved to Edmonton in mid-September and enrolled at the University of Alberta; I found a small basement apartment on Whyte Avenue near the campus. That November, I released

"Pen Pal Girl" and took the song to Lorne Thompson, a DJ at radio station CJCA, who hosted a popular teen show each evening entitled *Battle of the New Sounds*. Lorne scheduled my song to begin the competition on Monday evening against two other new songs; the winner was declared by the greatest number of call-ins during a one hour period. My friends and relatives were standing by their phones. From the word "Go" we kept the phones hot with our call-ins to the station. We won the first night! In fact, we won every night until the week was over! The next week, "Pen Pal Girl" was on the top twenty of the hit parade. The win brought about the usual hoop-la over the phenomenon of a local talent winning the week-long *Battle of the New Sounds*, and I was featured with an interview and picture in the *Edmonton Journal*, and a TV appearance on a popular teen show. But like all pop songs, in two months the song had faded from the scene.

## MOVING ON WITH LIFE

In the summer of 1963, after I completed my first year of university, I came to a fork in my road of life. I was hired by Standard Gravel to work for their survey crew at Milk River in southern Alberta. They were in need of a rod man. A rod man carried the measuring rod for the instrument man to shoot an elevation every twenty feet along cross-sections of the road or where the ground abruptly changed elevation; chains were moved forward at intervals of one hundred feet along the original or completed road. This job meant plenty of exercise, walking along the measuring chains to give instrument shots, and signalling with my arms to indicate distances. I was given some hurried survey experience on the road job at Newbrook, and soon I was gripping the steering wheel of the company's red GMC pickup and motoring along Highway 2, by-passing

Red Deer, through the centre of Calgary, past Lethbridge, and on to join our survey crew just outside Milk River near the Alberta-Montana border. For a nineteen year old kid from the wet parklands of north-central Alberta, the big sky and the hot prairie sun seemed to shrivel every pore in my body.

I had time to think about life in Milk River. There wasn't much entertainment in the long rolling hills of southern Alberta, especially if you didn't join the drinking brawls across the U.S. border at Coutts. The construction crew lived in a trailer camp, and I became friends with the operator of a bulldozer who was training to become a Roman Catholic priest. He played the mandolin, and when we weren't joining other guitar players and singers for evening jam sessions, we had some philosophical discussions about life and where we were going. He was a wonderful man of character, and was an example of how to respond with grace to the occasional ribbing crude construction men might direct at him because of his faith. On weekends I worked in the office for the time keeper, so I was busy and not tempted to engage in the cross-border shenanigans that we heard about on Monday mornings.

My second year of university was definitely a watershed. First of all, I moved into Grandma and Grandpa Stebner's upstairs apartment at 10526 - 80th Avenue. My course load was much different and more interesting. Second year education students enrolled in practical courses to learn about the various methods and curricula they would be teaching in the elementary classrooms. Furthermore, they were assigned two schools where they spent three weeks in each practice teaching in a classroom. Dad and Mom had been generous and gracious to give me their 1954 Ford car, so I could drive to the schools for my student teaching. I knew teaching was for me, because I loved motivating and instructing students, and I excelled in the classroom.

I had the privilege of teaming up with two wonderful female student teachers who also excelled. The first was a Roman Catholic nun who wore the traditional Roman Catholic habit. How amusing it must have been for bystanders and pedestrians to watch the sister and me speed along the street in our red-topped Ford to our grade-three teaching assignment at the Roman Catholic school!

## MUSIC CAREER HITS ROAD BLOCK

I still hadn't given up on releasing a recording for the Hit Parade. After university classes finished in the spring, I began singing on a part time basis with the Flamingos and performed nightly for a week with the band at the Edmonton Exhibition Bandstand. However, I wasn't happy with the choice of songs the leader chose for me; I decided the only way to sing my style of music as a recording artist was to write my own songs. I'd written a pretty love song that I entitled "Loving You." I booked the CKUA studio to record the song with the Flamingos and three back ground voices and was able to get a good sounding product. The band and I thought "Loving You" had potential, but we needed two songs—one for each side of a 45 recording. I wanted to get a lead on a record company before I proceeded, so I let the song sit on the shelf.

I decided later that winter to try recording two new songs I had written. Lorne Thompson of CJCA encouraged me to believe these songs had potential. I invited the Nomads to record with me—they were the best teen band in Edmonton at that time. We already had one local hit, "Pen Pal Girl," so the Nomads agreed to record a second time and look for a bigger record company with wider distribution. We recorded "Everyone Knows," and "Penny, Penny." We were pleased with our finished product, and a major record company indicated interest. Our hopes were dashed, however, when we discovered another road block. Record companies were hesitant about releasing new songs because another musical phenomenon was sweeping the popular teen scene—the Beatles! We would have to wait, which meant our songs wouldn't get aired. It's interesting to note in retrospect, however, that two of my recordings received recognition much later in my life. "Pen Pal Girl" was played on the CBC radio show, *Definitely Not the Opera* (February 12, 2011), and was included with "Loving You" on *Canada Rock Archives, Volume 1*, distributed by SuperOldies.com (2014).

## ANOTHER CALLING

Around this time another calling and conviction was beginning to grip my life when I became involved with the Edmonton Standard Church. Since my music career was on the shelf for the time being, I began to make friends with the small youth group and attended Sunday services at the little church on 91st Street. I knew God was drawing me away from the popular music scene and closer to Him, but I was still hesitant to trust Him entirely with my life.

The Reverend Russell and Verna Clarke had become the pastors at the Edmonton Standard Church and became influential in my faith life. They had been missionaries to China for many years with the Inland China Mission and had many stories of faith from their years of ministry among the Chinese people. They were patient and kind, offering counsel and support as I struggled to find God's will.

## TRANSITION YEAR

Year three of university was my best and most enjoyable. I had learned important study habits and how to discipline my time. I was also growing spiritually and attending the Standard Church on Sunday mornings. One of the courses I'd taken during my previous year at the U of A was Elementary School Music, where I learned how to direct a school choir and lead music. This training became useful when the Reverend Clarke asked me to lead worship services at our church. Each week I chose the hymns and led the congregational singing.

After university recessed that spring, I enrolled in two summer courses to work toward completing my B.Ed. Before summer classes began, however, I found temporary spring employment at Long Lake Provincial Park. My job was to help keep the park beautiful for the hundreds of tourists and campers who flocked to the beach during northern Alberta's short summer. I kept busy painting picnic tables, raking sand at the beach, forking piles of lawn grass, and cleaning shelters and toilets. The park was only twelve miles from our Balsam Grove farm, so I stayed at home with Mom and Dad in the new bungalow they had just built.

Living at Newbrook enabled me to attend Newbrook camp meeting. I'd been seriously contemplating where my life was going and where God fit into my plans. Pastor Nelson Peters from Ivanhoe, Ontario, was the evangelist. He was a simple but engaging preacher who usually cited a text and then told stories of faith about his life as a farmer and preacher. I was determined to make my peace with God, so one night during the camp I knelt at one of the wooden benches and made Jesus the Lord of my life. At that moment, life took on a different meaning.

During the spring of 1965, I applied to the Edmonton Public School Board to teach part time during the following school year while I enrolled in two university courses. I was accepted and assigned an eight-tenths position teaching grade six at Glendale Public School in Jasper Place at the west end of Edmonton. This proved to be a valuable year for my teaching career. During the previous year at the U of A, I'd enrolled in a course, Physical Education in the Elementary School, which taught a new method, highly touted in England, for instructing educational gymnastics. When Glendale and neighbouring schools acquired a new apparatus of bars and ropes for use in their Physical Education program, most elementary teachers were in a quandary about how to use the equipment. I was recruited to demonstrate lessons using the new apparatus. The superintendent of elementary Physical Education, Miss Audrey Allen, attended my demonstration and soon pigeon holed me as someone she could call on to demonstrate the new direction elementary P.E. was taking.

After another two courses during the summer, I graduated from the University of Alberta with my B.Ed. and accepted a teaching position at Hazeldean Public School with a grade four and five class. Miss Allen kept in touch with me, and I was honoured to teach a demonstration class in educational gymnastics at the Greater Edmonton Teachers' Convention for Northern Alberta on February 23, 1967, during Canada's Centennial celebrations, at the Ross Shepherd Composite High School. My class and I performed well and were invited to further demonstrate the new instructional methods in Calgary during the Easter break. Unfortunately, it was too difficult to recruit and transport my class to Calgary during the holidays. Besides, I was invited by the Reverend Ken Bombay to join him as soloist on his Easter week youth crusade across British Columbia, and I was eager for this experience.

Attending the Edmonton Standard Church had connected me to some people who were instrumental in changing my life. Charlie "Tremendous" Jones has a favourite saying, "You are the same today as you'll be in five years except for two things—the people you meet and the books you read." That was the case in my life. I was reading the Bible and Christian books that were changing my thought life, and I also met two influential people who impacted the ultimate direction of my life—Ken and Joan Bombay. When Marilyn Walker and Gunter Salzmann asked me to sing at their wedding ceremony, I was introduced to Ken Bombay. Ken was a Bible teacher at North West Bible College and a charismatic evangelist with the Pentecostal Assembles of Canada.

Becoming friends with the Bombays also introduced me to students at North West Bible College, and I was surrounded by young men and women who were called to Christian ministry. Hanging out with students like James Thomas and Dennis Sunderland, who were following God's call on their lives, made me consider God's call on my life. James had been a manager in a grocery store, and Dennis had been a pre-med student in university. Both had forsaken their secular careers to follow Jesus into ministry.

Instead of demonstrating educational gymnastics, I spent my Easter holidays travelling with Ken across the province of B.C. Each evening at various rallies he preached and I sang, including during the climax weekend at Glad Tidings Church in Vancouver. God was giving me a taste of ministry that was tugging at my heart.

My teaching career at Hazeldean became the greatest battle point of my life. I loved my class, but I was fighting a call to Christian ministry. My brother, Marvin, had graduated from high school the previous year with his senior matriculation but had decided to attend our denominational Bible School in Brockville, and I felt God calling me in the same direction.

### INTERLUDE: BABY SISTER

An unexpected blessing came into our family in the spring of 1966. I drove home one day from Edmonton and entered the

New baby sister, Karen, provided our family with many happy days of enjoyment apart from the heavy drudgery and chores on the homestead farm.

new farm house. All was quiet inside. Both Mom and Dad had gone to the barn to attend to some chores. Unexpectedly, I was aware that I was not alone in the house. Strangely, I found a crib set up. What was this all about? Walking over to the crib, I saw the cutest baby girl lying awake. She had reddish blond hair, blue eyes, and when she saw me, her little face lit up with the brightest smile—like she was so happy to see me! She won my heart immediately, and I quickly found Mom and Dad to find out what was going on. You could tell they wanted to know what I thought of this little girl. I said, "She's beautiful!" It wasn't long before I learned they would like to keep her and adopt her as their own daughter. I thought it was a wonderful idea. They began the process, and soon our family of boys had a new sister, Karen. She was a blessing to both Mom and Dad, but especially to Dad, who always wanted a girl who would sit on his knees and hug him—which Karen did incessantly. As Karen grew, Dad and Karen had a special relationship. I felt released from the emotional care of Mom and Dad with their attention focused on their new daughter.

## BROCKVILLE BIBLE COLLEGE

My battle over entering Christian ministry continued until one Sunday evening at Central Pentecostal Church in Edmonton. That night I knelt in a corner of the prayer room and told God I would follow Him wherever He would lead. It was then that the Reverend Ken Bombay found his way to where I was kneeling and placed his hand on my head and prayed to God that I would find His will for my life. That was the moment I said, "Yes," to God, and my life from that moment took a radically different path from which I had been pursuing.

Shortly after this event, I spoke with my mother and later to both of my parents about my desire to attend Brockville Bible College with Marvin that fall. I took a leave of absence from the Edmonton Public School Board and said good-bye to Hazeldean School—the most difficult decision I ever made in my life.

## LEGACY

God is always up to something that is bigger and more expansive that we can ever imagine. Little did I know while attending university that God was preparing me for something beyond teaching in a public school; I enrolled in courses that taught the basics of song leading, how to become an engaging public speaker, and what it takes to prepare lessons that are easy to follow and understand. I would use all of these skills when I eventually became the pastor of a local church. Nor was it simply coincidence that the Reverend Clarke recruited me to lead worship at the Edmonton Standard Church, or that Marilyn Walker requested me to sing at her wedding where I met Ken and Joan Bombay; these were divine appointments God used to nudge me in the direction He'd planned for my life. God even used my experience with secular bands to prepare me to eventually sing and record gospel music that would minister to hundreds of people.

I've learned that God is progressive, always working ahead of us, providing experiences, introducing us to people, leading and pulling us forward to find His perfect will. My prayer is that my readers and family will recognize how God uses everything—family roots, past experiences, and significant people—to prepare us for future ministry—many times beyond our wildest dreams.

Paul understood this when he wrote, "*And we know that in all things God works for the good of those who love him, who have been called according to his purpose*" (Romans 8:28).

# Chapter Six

# Marriage, Ministry, and Mission

"For I know the plans I have for you," declares the Lord, "plans to prosper you and not to harm you, plans to give you hope and a future."

—Jeremiah 29:11

## CENTENNIAL CELEBRATIONS

Nineteen-sixty-seven was one of the most notable years in Canadian history because it was Canada's Centennial, and celebrations were held throughout the nation. The year was also a watershed in my life, because it was when I decided to follow God's call to enter the ministry of the Standard Church. That fall, Marvin and I pointed the '54 Ford Customline eastward along the Trans-Canada Highway and began the long, arduous drive to Brockville Bible College. We looked forward to a year of excitement and challenge with new horizons before us, confident that God was leading. One of our first stops along the way was in Medicine Hat to eat Mom's freshly fried chicken that she had lovingly packed for our journey. Little did we know that some years later Mom and Dad would be living in Medicine Hat in their retirement years near Darrell and his family.

After many dreary miles of driving through the bush and around the lakes of northern Ontario, our first destination was Ivanhoe, Ontario. We arrived in time to sing and lead worship at the historic Ivanhoe Camp Meeting near Madoc, Ontario. The Reverend Eldon Craig, a young budding Standard Church pastor and preacher, was the evangelist, I was the song leader, and Marvin sang with the Brockville Bible College Quartet. I took particular notice of the quartet's piano player, Faye Montgomery, who was also returning for her second year of studies at BBC.

When camp was over, Marvin and I had a few days to tour before college opened. We joined Ross Hobin in Brockville and rode with him to Montreal to attend Expo 67, which was magnificently displayed on the Ile of Notre-Dame. Ross parked his car at his grandmother Conley's home, and we rode the subway (my first experience on a subway) to the World's Fair that served as the focal point for Canada's one hundredth birthday celebrations. We joined the throngs of people wandering among the impressive pavilions and exhibitions displaying cultures, products, and foods from around the world. That evening we stayed with Grandmother Conley before heading back to Brockville and the Bible College the next day.

## FIRST PASTORATE

Before arriving in Ontario, I had contacted the Reverend Conley, superintendent of the Standard Church, and volunteered to fill a pulpit during the year if there was an opening. I was appointed to Wilton and Violet, a small country circuit of two churches a few miles west of Kingston, near Odessa, Ontario. I would preach and pastor on the weekend and study at Brockville Bible College during the week. The church members were especially kind and adopted Marvin and me as their western sons, serving us many after-church dinners and lunches each weekend.

Carmel and Lyle Lasher lived near the Violet parsonage, and on many occasions we stopped by for lunch and listened to stories of Carmel's father, the Reverend George Kelly, who had ministered as pastor and evangelist in the early days of the Standard Church. I also remember listening to one of his sermons on reel-to-reel tape entitled, "The Potter's Wheel," and the effect his message and preaching had on me as a twenty-three-year-old preacher. Pauline and Allan Dafoe became a second mother and dad to us two Alberta boys while we were so far away from home, and made certain we didn't eat alone on Sunday after church. We feasted on many roast beef dinners at the Dafoe's, watched the popular television evangelist, Rex Humbard, and listened to Pauline's stories of her dad, the Reverend Nelson Peters, a converted farmer and icon in Standard Church circles during the '50s and '60s. He had been instrumental in my own decision to follow Jesus at Newbrook Camp Meeting. Many others provided hospitality and love, but I must not fail to mention Mrs. Marjorie Chiles and her apple pies—they were never-to-be-forgotten fabulous and famous. She and her husband, Leslie, also took Marvin and me into their home on many occasions to "feed and fuss" over us.

Every Sunday I preached, sang, and exhorted the congregation to follow Jesus, and they responded positively. My first pastorate was like a preacher's honeymoon, and I would need that encouragement and affirmation to face the battles ahead.

## BIBLE COLLEGE DAYS

College life during the first three days of the week was hectic but exciting. I had opportunity not only to study the Bible with the Reverends Elgan Armstrong and Earl Conley, but also to form friendships with students from across our church. I also began to take greater notice of Faye Montgomery and form a friendship with her. Campus extra-curricular activities had another plus—I was provided with opportunities to satisfy my love for singing and music. Not only were there numerous musical jamming sessions, but I also formed a trio with my brother, Marvin, and Ross Hobin. I also led a small college choral that sang for the college on deputation work in the churches. Our BBC music that year was so enthusiastically received by people and churches that we decided to release a recording, *The Joy of Living*, featuring songs by our popular quartet (Elsie Barnard, Margo Crozier, Faye Montgomery, Ross Hobin, and Marvin Croswell), as well as numbers by our choral, men's trio, and a solo by me. How exciting it was to travel to Kitchener, Ontario and record with Calvary Records!

Each weekend I preached and called on the Wilton-Violet parishioners who received me with open and enthusiastic arms, but deep in my heart I knew this wonderful rural pastorate was not my life calling. I had a deep conviction that God wanted me in Brockville with the college church. I was a teacher and educator. I knew I must resign my role as pastor to these wonderful people and did so in the spring of 1968. I determined to wait on God's timing for Brockville, but the opportunity came soon. The present pastor, Eldon Craig, his wife, Francis, and their two girls, Sharon and Merri-Lynn, had been temporarily stationed at the Brockville church in 1967 while waiting to sail to Egypt as the first on-field-missionaries since Earl and Doris Conley had returned in 1961. The Craigs left for Egypt in November of 1968, and I was appointed interim pastor to continue the next Sunday. I resigned my position with the Edmonton School Board with much reticence and nostalgia to accept the appointment, but a call of God was on my heart, so I cut ties with my teaching career in Alberta.

## BROCKVILLE STANDARD CHURCH

When Marvin had finished his courses at Brockville Bible College in the spring of 1968 and returned to Edmonton to enroll at the University of Alberta, I stayed behind to complete my year of pastoring at Wilton and Violet. How lonely it was to watch his car turn up the Brockville Bible College driveway and onto Perth Street toward Alberta and realize we would never experience a year of serving this closely again! I had prepared mentally to assume the pastorate of the Brockville Standard Church when the time came available, complete more Bible courses, and continue to lead a Bible college choral.

The Brockville Standard Church was a challenge. The congregation was small, but it was the college church for the student body. The property had been purchased at 100 Perth Street in 1923, a small postage stamp-sized city lot across the railroad tracks from the ten acre Bible College campus and market garden. The building was constructed from hand-made cement blocks. There was on-site-parking for about five cars at the side and rear if they squeezed in tightly; a hydro pole had been placed about one-third of the way across the driveway to complicate driving in or backing out onto Perth Street. The only reason given for not building on the spacious Brockville Bible College property was that the south side of the railroad tracks represented being urban inside the city limits of Brockville, and the north side represented being rural. The Brockville Standard Church wished to be urban.

I was full of enthusiasm but extremely naive. The small wage offered was no deterrence to me. I sensed a definite "call," so I simply found a half-time job at the local Prince of Wales Public School teaching the boys' physical education program from grades four to eight. In retrospect, this was one of the best things I could have done to help further our ministry. Overseeing the entire boys' physical education program was a challenge that my training in educational gymnastics had not prepared me for, but my principal, Mr. David Cotie, was patient in supporting me, and I had three good years in that position (concluded by our school winning the 1971 trophy for the Leeds Grenville County Junior Track Meet).

The next year I was assigned a grade three class at the historic Brock school (a satellite of POW); it was the only year I taught full time in Brockville and did so to qualify for my permanent Ontario teaching certificate. I'm thankful for the twenty-four years I eventually taught at Prince of Wales. God was good. Thirteen teachers from POW attended our church at one time or another during my teaching career, including my principal, David Cotie, and his wife, Bea. They later became members of our church and personal friends. Moreover, my part time teaching job helped support our family during the building years at the church, allowing us to remain long term in Brockville without personal financial stress while we led and guided the congregation though the various stages of growth and development. Suffice it to say, I am a strong advocate of "tent-making" ministries for young pastors seeking to plant new churches or grow small churches.

## FAYE MONTGOMERY

During my second year at Brockville Bible College, I began to date and court Faye Montgomery. She was a talented young woman from Foresters Falls, Ontario. She had graduated from BBC and was enrolled in Ottawa Teachers' College. I was intrigued with her, because she had a warm personality and a wonderful supportive family. She was popular with everyone and was highly intelligent. She even won awards for her academic performance. Furthermore, I thought she was beautiful! I wasn't quite certain how to make an impression on her; I'd already "goofed" a date by taking her on a "surprise flight" over Brockville and the St. Lawrence Valley in a small rented airplane. I didn't know that Faye was averse to flying. The flight didn't impress her, but she was too polite to indicate her nausea from dipping, banking, and gliding over the St. Lawrence River and the city of Brockville. Nevertheless, after repeatedly dating Faye in Ottawa while she attended teachers' college, I drove her home one evening to visit her parents in Foresters Falls. In the summer kitchen of the old Ottawa Valley farmhouse, I built up enough courage to ask Faye if she might consider becoming my wife. To my surprise, she accepted my proposal!

The next day we drove to Ottawa, and as we walked together in one of the beautifully landscaped parks I was in a daze, but Faye seemed calm and assured. We soon spoke to Faye's parents, Bert and Evelyn, to get their blessing for our marriage, and began to make plans for a June wedding after Faye graduated from teacher's college, where she obtained the highest academic average in her class.

We were married on June 28, 1969, on a hot, humid day in the Foresters Falls United Church by the Reverend Sylvester MacDonald and the Reverend George Armstrong. Mom and Dad drove from Alberta with Karen, Marvin, and Darrell to "The Falls." It was a wonderful celebration of our marriage, and we had a typical "valley" wedding supper of roast turkey with all the trimmings in the Foresters Falls United Church

Laurence Croswell and Faye Montgomery, a happy couple on their
wedding day, in Foresters Falls, Ontario, June 28, 1969.

basement hall. There were many special people who attended,
including my principal and his wife, David and Bea Cotie. Elgan Armstrong offered one of his hilariously humorous toasts
to the bride, and Faye and I set out together on a life partnership of faith, family, and ministry.

## MINISTRY IN BROCKVILLE

When Annual Conference was held in the spring of 1969, the
stationing committee appointed me to continue as pastor of
the Brockville Standard Church. They were quite aware that I
was soon to be married to Faye Montgomery, and the Kingston
Conference superintendent, the Reverend Arnold Rigby, indicated he believed in our ministry potential. He did his utmost

to encourage us in every way possible. Our gratitude to him will not be forgotten.

The Brockville church was a challenge. George Armstrong had been pastor of the church from 1962 to 1966. He'd been a tireless Sunday school worker and used his car to bring children to the church from the city and countryside. Sunday school attendance rose to more than sixty, and new people began to attend. When the Reverend Armstrong was stationed in Napanee, the Reverend J. B. Pring temporarily filled in until the Conference of 1967 when the Reverend Eldon and Frances Craig were assigned to pastor the church while preparing for the Egyptian mission field. Eldon and Francis began reaching out to the young couples who had begun to attend the church, and about five couples began to take leadership roles and serve. The Armstrongs and Craigs were responsible for beginning the transition of the Brockville Standard Church from primarily serving the BBC staff and students into a church that reached into the broader community.

When I began my ministry in Brockville, I was busy to say the least. I was teaching half time at POW public school, finishing my Bible college courses for ordination, getting the parsonage at 28 Schofield Avenue ready for a new bride, and teaching an English course as well as leading the small college choral at BBC. Moreover, I began to study and implement the strategy of emphasizing Sunday school as a means for outreach and expanding our ministry in the hinterland and city of Brockville. As I look back, I don't know how I kept up my schedule!

After Faye and I were married, I continued to be involved in the college ministry with Elgan and Verda Armstrong, the principal and administrators of BBC. Faye taught kindergarten at Maynard Public School and arranged a children's church ministry on Sunday during the preaching portion of the service so the adults and youth wouldn't be distracted, and the children might learn more about Jesus and Christian living.

The college, though small, was flourishing (in 1969–1970 attendance reached a peak of thirty students), and the church was growing. The Armstrongs recognized the need for a strong local church to attract students, and in turn were extremely helpful in the Brockville church. Verda played the new Hammond organ, giving the church a completely different atmosphere, and Elgan applied his building expertise and headed up major renovations and modernization of the church sanctuary. Soon a couple of new younger families and couples were attracted to the little church on Perth Street and joined our congregation.

Outreach and evangelism for many evangelical churches in the 1960s was highly influenced by Dr. Jack Hyles, Pastor of a large church in Hammond, Indiana. I had read his books and travelled with BBC to attend the International Sunday School Conventions in Detroit. Bus ministry was promoted as an effective means for church growth. Believing that we could do it too, I purchased a previously owned Pontiac station wagon and soon filled it with children. About two years later, we purchased a used school bus. Mike Smith painted it green, and soon we were bringing over thirty children and youth to the church on Perth Street. We were grateful for dedicated drivers who manoeuvred the bus along the country lanes and city streets, while I served as bus captain, running to doors gathering my bus congregation safely on board, singing Sunday School choruses to keep everyone engaged and happy, and handing out treats when the riders returned after church. Jill Montgomery (no relationship to Faye) was a dedicated high school volunteer who faithfully helped on the bus each Sunday. The new children, however, upset the status quo of the church, not to mention that it surprised many in our congregation that on rally Sundays there might be one hundred in attendance (on one Sunday 150)—many of them wiggling, unchurched children and youth with little experience in church protocol.

Two of our most gifted teachers, Mary Wilson and Helen Wiltse, taught overflowing classes during the Sunday school hour in the middle of the basement or in the newly built balcony; my youth class met behind the furnace room. Faye and her staff of inexperienced youth somehow conducted the children's church without major incidents in the basement while I preached the message in the upstairs sanctuary. I never conducted the services much over one hour, or I might have had a riot on my hands! Moreover, a noon-time freight train might rumble by on the tracks a block to the north, the wig wags clanging loudly like an alarm to indicate that it was time to end the service. Only God could have protected us and all those children from incidents in the church or accidents with the bus.

Every Sunday when I arrived home about 1:00 p.m. after picking up bus children, teaching the youth class, leading the worship, preaching the message, and finally riding the bus to take children home, I was exhausted! But God blessed and the church was growing. There was a new sense of excitement and anticipation about the Brockville Standard Church.

We realized, however, that in order for the church to experience continued growth and expansion, we would eventually need to move from our Perth Street location. In 1975, the church purchased a three-and-a-half acre lot from Mr. Bill Van Dusen just outside the city limits on County Road 27, the extension of Centennial Road leading to Lyn. We planned to relocate the parsonage and build a church that would seat approximately two hundred people, but with adequate off street parking that did not involve a hydro pole blocking the entrance.

## THE EARLY YEARS: FAITH AND FAMILY

There are times when Faye and I look back at the early years in our marriage and ministry and simply sigh, wondering how we could have been involved in so much—teaching, singing, leading, building, preaching, visiting, studying, and riding on a Sunday school bus!

Faye taught kindergarten classes for five years at Maynard Public School, until one day when we learned some exciting news—she was pregnant! We were still living in the parsonage at 28 Schofield Avenue, so we prepared a small bedroom to become the nursery. How excited we were on the morning of November 2, 1974, as we quickly drove to the Brockville General Hospital where Dr. Dunn delivered a squirming, wide-eyed baby boy. We named him Mark Aaron Croswell. We thought he was the most beautiful baby in the whole world!

What joy Mark brought to Faye and me. Mark changed our lives. We could no longer just think about ourselves, but we had to consider the responsibilities of a family. We began to ponder what our future might hold and how we would provide for this newborn son. Soon Grandma Montgomery arrived to see the new grandbaby and help Faye in the early weeks of mother care; then Grandma Croswell flew in from Alberta to see her new grandson and lend a helping hand. Mark was the first grandchild on both sides of his family, so he was very special. He was an active baby, sometimes not prone to easily falling asleep, especially when he was out of routine (which made it difficult at times since we were pastors and very much in the public). There were occasions when we drove him around the block once or twice to help him relax and go to sleep, especially after an evening Bible study or church service. If we needed a babysitter we called on Donna Rae Armstrong, who seemed to have just the right touch and personality for Mark. We were

Bert and Evelyn Montgomery, Faye's parents, enjoyed talking about their farms with Leonard and Ella Croswell, Laurence's parents, while visiting in Brockville.

never afraid to leave him should we have an appointment or call that needed to be made.

Life was soon to change again. When Mark was six months old, our church sold the parsonage at 28 Schofield with the goal to rebuild a new home on our Centennial Road location. We temporarily moved into the one bedroom apartment, just below Helen Wiltse, that was part of the girls' dorm on the Bible College campus. It was cramped, and Mark's crib was located next to our bed. We lived in the apartment for a year and a half. Our accommodations were crowded, but we had some good times living so near the Armstrongs and the college students.

As Mark grew to be a toddler, he became intrigued with Harold Moyles, the college gardener. Mark would do his best to pronounce Harold's name and imitate the tractor sound when he would see Harold drive by with his big red tractor

Family Portrait taken on Darrell and Linda Croswell's wedding day,
July 31, 1982. Seated: Leonard and Ella Croswell
Standing L to R: Marvin, Karen, Darrell, Laurence
Their family is grateful for their parent's legacy of hard work and sacrifice.

and corn wagon. Mom and Dad visited us that summer from Alberta, and we had a wonderful family reunion with my parents and Faye's mother and dad. Our parents thoroughly enjoyed each other's company, since they all had been farmers and had much in common.

In the fall of 1976, we moved to the new parsonage on Centennial Road. Ross Armstrong had been the contractor, and we were pleased with the Tudor-style brick house he built. We were also grateful to leave the cramped apartment on Perth Street and enter the spanking new home in the woods, but there were adjustments to make. Now, instead of living in close proximity to our dorm neighbours and the busy life of college we had grown accustomed to, we were separated and isolated in the woods. Our new house was situated in a clearing, surrounded by sugar maples, sturdy oaks, and wild apple trees;

the house was reached by turning off Centennial Road onto a winding leafy laneway that began with a sharp incline and then curved through the trees before reaching the driveway that led to the attached garage.

The natural surroundings were beautiful but secluded. Winter snowstorms filled the snaking laneway with drifts and ice, which often made entering or leaving by car difficult and precarious—especially when I needed to be at school for a morning class at Prince of Wales. I purchased an ancient Cockshutt 30 tractor with an archaic bucket to move snow and clear the laneway for our car. I had more troubles with that tractor, starting it and operating the bucket, than it was worth! We made it through the first winter with only minor road hazards, and rejoiced when the sun warmed and the snow began to recede and disappear. Soon we were inhaling the pleasing fragrances of wild apple blossoms and purple lilacs that marked the beginning of spring. Our Centennial Road haven became a veritable Garden of Eden, carpeted with multi-coloured anemones and white trilliums.

## THE NEW COMPLEX

As the local church grew and we partnered more closely with BBC, a larger vision began to emerge. Why not combine the assets of Brockville Bible College and the church headquarters with the local church, and cooperatively build a facility that would be larger than anything we had attempted in the Standard Church before? Everyone would benefit. We had a dream and a vision, and soon we were negotiating with Bill Van Dusen for a forty acre strip of land beside and behind the new church lot on Centennial Road. He offered it to us for $71,000, a great deal of money for the denomination in 1977. Elgan Armstrong engaged an artist to draw a visionary concept of an ultramodern building complex that would house the denominational head-quarters, the Bible College, and the local church. Earl Conley, our General Superintendent, passionately shared the vision at the annual Feast of Pentecost, and gifts and pledges were received. Applications and minor variances to accommodate a church and college were made to the Elizabethtown Township, and on August 11, 1978, the deal was signed. The Standard Church became owner of a large parcel of land on Centennial Road, with a dream of becoming a teaching-administrative centre that would also become home to a vibrant local church reaching out to the greater St. Lawrence Valley. The vision became known as the "New Complex."

Three years after the new parsonage was built on Centennial Road, we began construction of Phase One of the New Complex in the summer of 1979. The cement block church on Perth Street was sold to the Seventh Day Adventists, and our new church was built on the newly purchased denominational land. Elgan Armstrong was the designer and contractor. It was a very different style of church building. The auditorium, located on the second floor, was accessed by sloping ramps; the design of the building looked for-all-the-world like a Holiday Inn Motel, but it was only the first phase of what was to be a "three phase project." We moved into the new sanctuary by November 1979, and the church was dedicated on January 13, 1980. It was a new day for our church. It created a "spiritual buzz" in our community, and by 1985, the relocated church was topping attendances of 250. Our motto was: "Reaching and teaching the St. Lawrence Valley—for Jesus' sake!"

## NEW FAMILY MEMBER

By 1981, we had comfortably settled into our home and surroundings on Centennial Road, but we longed to add to our family. Mark was six and wanted a brother. How happy and blessed we were on the morning of September 12, 1981, to drive to the Brockville General Hospital a second time, and, again with the assistance of Dr. Dunn, safely welcome a second son, Darren Jonathan Croswell. I shall not forget the day we brought Darren home. Our family sat on the chesterfield and admired this new baby and simply enjoyed the moment. As Faye held this newest member of our family in her arms, Mark and I sat beside her, one on each side, our faces beaming with joy, looking into little Darren's eyes. Faye murmured, "I just want him to be perfect!" As far as we were concerned he was perfect, and we thanked God for such a precious gift.

## ENTHUSIASM FOR COMPLEX WANES, BUT CHURCH PROSPERS

Shortly after the land on Centennial Road was purchased, enthusiasm across our denomination for the New Complex began to sputter. Prospective students to BBC began to look elsewhere for larger Bible colleges with greater course selections and wider opportunities. In the fall of 1983, BBC president Elgan Armstrong resigned, and a driving force for completion of the New Complex dream was removed. Attendance at BBC dwindled. For the remainder of the year, I served as interim college president to help students finish their college term. The following year, the Reverend Wayne Briggs, who had been pastor of the Brockville Wesleyan Church, was appointed Bible college dean and took over leadership of the struggling student body. The Reverend Briggs became a healing balm to many in the Bible college and the Standard Church denomination; he travelled to churches and camp meetings counselling pastors and lay people alike.

Despite the fact that college enrolment had declined, our local Standard Church was flourishing. Our vision for the church was greatly enlarged. With the loss of student numbers, the Bible college and headquarters began to make concrete plans to relocate to Centennial Road as well, because it made financial sense. On January 10, 1985, the General Executive of the Standard Church voted unanimously to sell the existing Bible college properties and cooperate with the local church to build phase two in return for classroom and office space, and to make room for a library and bookstore. The board sold the principal's residence on Convey Crescent during the summer and rebuilt a new home on the Centennial Road campus for the new dean and his wife, Wayne and Pat Briggs.

In 1986, Brockville Standard Church began to make plans with the denomination to build the second phase of the New Complex. The remaining BBC buildings, consisting of the girls' dorm and Bishop Ralph Horner's historic, seventy-five-year-old administrative building at 243 Perth Street, were sold to facilitate the transfer to Centennial Road. The new addition was completed in 1989, and our first Sunday service was celebrated on December 10; we were blessed with a record attendance of 425. An interior designer had been hired to suggest possibilities for interior décor that would be pleasing in arrangement, style, and colours; creatively patterned carpet was installed, providing for individual seating arranged in a semicircle around a large corner stage fashioned with creative lighting and rich, hanging drapery. The ceiling was lowered, and the drab grey gym was transformed into a magnificent sanctuary, equipped with a professional sound system that created an ambiance for worship and praise. Few would recognize the new sanctuary as the ultimate gymnasium it would later become in 2005. Classes began to be taught in the existing first phase, and the college library was moved to the balcony of the new addition.

Phase Three of the new complex was completed in 2004—a beautiful sanctuary seating six hundred with a boulevard connecting all three phases into one complete facility. It was dedicated on January 30 by the former superintendent of the Standard Church, the Reverend George MacGarvey. I felt confident that we'd finally completed what God had called us to do in Brockville.

# Final Things

When Faye and I began our pastoral ministries in Brockville, we didn't expect to spend a lifetime in one church. After all, most Standard Church pastors remained about four years in their appointments, and if they stayed six years, that was considered a long time. Faye and I pastored the Brockville church for forty years!

Forty years represents a significant lifetime in the Bible. Moses lived for forty years as a pampered prince in Egypt. He was forty years old when he escaped from Pharaoh's sword to live in the wilderness of Midian. He spent another forty years learning the skills of a shepherd in the desert of Midian. The next forty years were spent leading the children of Israel through the wilderness of the Sahara in preparation to enter the Promised Land. Each forty year period was marked by miraculous interventions by God—the rescue of baby Moses by the Egyptian princess, God's calling at the burning bush, and ultimately God's monumental intervention and provision at the parting of the Red Sea. Leading the Children of Israel was no walk in the park! The Israelites were constantly murmuring, complaining, and questioning Moses' leadership, yet God graciously enabled Moses to form the Hebrew children into a formidable nation. When Moses passed the leadership baton to Joshua, they were ready to enter the land of Canaan.

Faye and I don't consider ourselves to be on a spiritual level with Moses; nevertheless, we pastored the Brockville Standard Church, which ultimately became Centennial Road Church, for forty years. We experienced God's miraculous deeds of provision. We celebrated and praised God with our congregation, and we also experienced the other side of the coin as we led our church through seasons of difficulty in the wilderness. We listened to murmuring and complaining, and, yes, watched outright rebellion—times when we could only pray and trust. There were seasons of triumph on the mountaintop when we rejoiced, and seasons of despair in the valley when we wondered if God even knew we existed. In fact, one evening I stood outside our parsonage at 28 Schofield and cried out to God, "Do you know where 28 Schofield is? It's right here, God! Can you see me?" But after forty years of ministry and trusting God, we can look back and say with Romans 8:28 that God caused all things *to work together for good*. What looked like unfavourable setbacks actually turned out to be God's setups for blessing and the ultimate furthering of His Kingdom. Many times, Faye and I watched God turn ashes of despair into songs of rejoicing. What amazed us was that each victory had little to do with our gifts or abilities—what we did or could do— but everything to do with the miraculous hand of God! The Brockville Standard Church was blessed by God and became the largest church in our denomination and one of the largest churches in Brockville. Only God could pull something like this off!

In 2004, the Standard Church voted to join the Central Canada District of the Wesleyan Church. Four years later on December 31, 2008, I resigned as senior pastor of CRSC. After our final service, Faye and I drove south for a restful January holiday in the sun of Florida. Returning that spring, we travelled for church services in Calgary and Edmonton. We visited my mother and family in Medicine Hat. Later in the church year, I was appointed zone leader and assistant district superintendent of Alberta for the Wesleyan Church.

I'm now involved in a ministry I never thought possible—mentoring pastors and assisting western churches in my home province of Alberta. We can truly say we have seen miracles take place as God has provided supernaturally and these churches have experienced revival and turnarounds as they are beginning to reach out and serve their communities.

## TRIBUTE TO DAD

Not many have the privilege of preaching their father's funeral message, but I did on October 23, 2003, at the Pattison's Funeral Home in Medicine Hat, Alberta. My Dad, Leonard William Croswell, was ninety-one years old when he passed from this earth. Mark, my son, read a eulogy tracing his grandfather's life from childhood in Saskatchewan and homesteading in Alberta, to his eventual retirement in Wetaskiwin and Medicine Hat. His daughter, Karen, and son, Marvin, spoke words of praise honouring his life, character, and accomplishments. His youngest son, Darrell, organized the arrangements with Pattison's and provided emotional support for Mom. I preached a message of challenge using Abraham's journey of faith to the Promised Land as my theme. It was a fitting tribute to a man who purchased a ten dollar homestead in the wilds of Balsam Grove and set out as a fourteen year old boy with axe in hand to clear the land, grub roots, and wrestle with a breaking plow behind a team of spirited horses. My dad had a dream. His homestead was a challenge, but he transformed the primitive forest and tangled brush into a productive farm to support and nourish his family; they in turn became successful citizens and made positive contributions to their respective communities and churches.

After the service, family and friends gathered at Hillcrest Church to fellowship and reminisce. Dad's younger brother, Walter, was there—his confidant, co-worker, and best friend. Nephews and nieces, grandchildren, and old friends renewed their acquaintances with one another. There was laughter and joy as we sipped coffee, tea, and punch, and helped ourselves to sandwiches and squares. Many took pictures to remember the day. It was the kind of party Dad would have enjoyed. The next morning, our family drove to the cemetery to bid Dad one final goodbye and place his body in the grave. With breaking voice, I read that one day we shall not all sleep, but when the Lord's trumpet sounds, the dead in Christ shall rise, and we shall all rise to meet the Lord in the air. We shall be with the Lord forever. These are words of comfort we cling to.

## TRIBUTE TO MOM

On February 2, 2015, twelve years after Dad's funeral, we repeated the same ritual when we laid my mother, Ella Stebner Croswell, to rest beside Dad in the same Medicine Hat cemetery. This time, however, all eight grandchildren were old enough to take part in the service at Pattison's, and each one either sang a song, read a scripture, gave words of tribute, or shared memories. We recalled how Mom, a little German girl from Poland, learned to speak and read English while attending grade one in the small town school at Leduc. She moved during the Depression with her family to a homestead south of Newbrook. Ella was the oldest child and was assigned chores and responsibilities as her parents began to chop and scratch out an existence on the new farm. She walked along the railroad track to the one room country school in town, ultimately graduating from grade eight. After marriage in 1943, she continued the daily grind of milking cows, planting a large garden, and canning vegetables and fruit as she joined Leonard on his emerging homestead— all to make ends meet and provide for her soon-to-arrive family. Ella Croswell's children and grandchildren are the recipients and benefactors of her unselfish labours and sacrifice. We were at the service to say thank you, we love you, and will always remember and appreciate you.

## END OF AN ERA

"See you in the morning." These were Mom's final words to Dad, kissing him before his stretcher was loaded aboard the waiting air ambulance. It was goodbye down here, but good morning in Heaven. Dad passed into the arms of Jesus on the flight to Calgary. Twelve years later, we laid Ella beside Leonard in the Medicine Hat Cemetery to wait for the sound of the trumpet and promise of resurrection morning. It was the end of an era. Homesteading days were over, but a new and glorious land was just ahead!

## LEGACY

Faye and I determined to serve God in our generation. We did our best to become part of building God's Kingdom in the St. Lawrence Valley. God had worked across the generations of our families and left us a legacy of faith in Jesus. We sensed a strong call to pastoral ministry; we desired to pass that faith along to our sons and their eventual families. Faye and I prayed together before our sons were born, and while our family was young we continued that habit. We included our sons in family worship. After the evening meal, we held our sons on our knees, and with arms wrapped around them, read a Bible story, discussed our day's activities, and prayed together. Faye was supportive and helpful in our devotional time, but I always felt it was my responsibility to lead and make certain that we reserved this time for our family's devotional worship.

There is a portion in the Bible that expresses my desire and determination. It was Joshua's farewell to the leaders and officials of Israel. He reminded them that not one of God's promises had failed. He encouraged them to honour God and serve Him with all faithfulness. He concluded with these words: "... *choose for yourselves this day whom you will serve ... But as for me and my household, we will serve the Lord*" (Joshua 24:15).

Laurence & Faye Croswell, with sons Darren and Mark, celebrating the
50th wedding anniversary of Leonard & Ella Croswell, August 9, 1992.